ANECDOTES OF AN ORCADIAN

TO PERU AND BACK

KEN SCOTT

2020

Front cover:
Photos of Howe Farm, Harray, Orkney and Machu Picchu, Peru.
The planet we all live on!
Flags of the Orkney Islands and Peru.

Final editing and cover design:
Alistair Scott (Ken's youngest brother)

Contents

ACKNOWLEDGEMENTS

I am writing as a missionary and not as a Christian apologist, so I wish to undergird everything that I articulate in this book by thanking God for His inspired Word contained in the Bible. My concern is with truth and I have a high view of Scripture as the inspired, God breathed, and inerrant Word of God.

Two wonderful truths in Scripture elicit my gratitude. Firstly, the substitutionary atonement of Christ's death on the cross, a "truth" that explains the godhead putting on human flesh and of Christ becoming the answer to our search for truth. I understand that anyone who does not have a sense of personal sin will not welcome the biblical doctrine of Christ's atoning death. This is at the centre of every Christian's faith.

The second truth I wish to thank God for is the gift of life freely given to us by God. We read Job's words (Job 1:21) as he mourns the death of his children: "I came naked from my mother's womb, and I will be naked when I leave. The Lord gave me what I had, and the Lord has taken it away. Praise the name of the Lord." Life belongs to God. Tragedies in life prompt us to repent of our sin and be ready at any time to die. I am reminded that my life is not my own, it is but a loan and will be taken away. In Christ, our lives have been "bought with a price", so we seek to glorify the Lord, because our time will be very soon.

This septuagenarian thanks the Lord for many who have contributed to making life a good one. The contents of this book have been written down during the United Kingdom "lockdown" due to the coronavirus, in March, April, and May in 2020. However, the events recorded represent a lifetime that led me from Orkney to Peru and back, and to other places along the way. I have been accompanied through life by Jeannie, my wife, and have been blessed by the arrival of our two children, Rebecca, and Samuel. In turn Rebecca and Ganesh, her husband, blessed us with our two lovely grandchildren, Anjali, and Ajay. Samuel has found love during this most difficult time. After the Lord, these, my family members, are my treasures.

I thank God for Orkney, my place of birth, for my parents, my upbringing on a farm, for my siblings, their loved ones, my education and, for more memories than I can recall. On a spiritual plane I am indebted to too many people to mention, but they include folk in Kirkwall Baptist Church, my unsolicited mentor (the late Jim Stockan), the Birmingham Bible Institute, my colleagues in Peru in the Regions Beyond Missionary Union (later part of Latin Link), colleagues and students in the Belfast Bible College, those in Baptist Missions, others in the Irish Baptist College, University lecturers and students and, brothers and sisters in Christ who became, and still are, my friends.

Jeannie and I shared membership in different churches; the Kirkwall Baptist Church, several Iglesia Evangélica Peruana churches in Peru, the Christian and Missionary Alliance Church in Lince, Lima, Newtownbreda Baptist Church and Baptist Churches in Tacna, Peru. Leaders and members became our friends and changed us for the better. Recently, Jeannie and I have continued to experience the wealth of fellowship proffered to us by the Revd Willie Nixon and his wife Caroline, and we have renewed fellowship with our friends the Rev Desi Maxwell and his wife Heather.

It is my belief that if someone has three good friends, that person is rich indeed. I think I can count on more than that but for fear of omitting some, whose influence has shaped these pages, I have opted to generalize. I do wish to include my appreciation to two friends for presenting the book: to Pastor Alan Baird and the Rev. Willie Nixon I owe you both my thanks. I acknowledge the input into my spiritual journey from colleagues, lecturers, pastors, students, Mission Directors, Americans, British, Peruvians and those of other nationalities. Any list would be incomplete. To one and all my thanks.

Where does one start and where does one stop? Books, sermons, classes, lectures, and life experiences have all enriched my life and have contributed to this short volume. I am including material, original to me, but must admit that my reflective comments are never exclusively mine. I do not always know the distinction between what my experience was or whether I imbibed thinking from others, but I wish to claim that everything included, I made to be mine. My thanks to Jeannie, my wife, for editing my Scottish! My youngest brother, Alistair, deserves acknowledgement for preparing the book for publishing. Nevertheless, I accept full responsibility for the content of this book and for its limitations.

Everyone has a story to tell and I do not want to be pretentious in writing a selection of anecdotes and reflections as if mine are more important than others. My desire is to make the statement that Jesus Christ is the person at the centre of my life. He is the only one who makes sense of everything for me. Just a few words of praise from the last book of the Bible serve to focus why Jesus Christ is unique above everyone:

> *Holy, holy, holy is the Lord God, the Almighty--- the one who always was, who is, and who is still to come.*
>
> *You are worthy, O Lord our God, to receive glory and honour and power. For you created all things, and they exist because you created what you pleased.*
>
> *You are worthy to take the scroll and break its seal and open it. For you were slaughtered, and your blood has ransomed people for God from every tribe and language and people and nation. And you have caused them to become a Kingdom of priests for our God. And they will reign on the earth.*
>
> *Worthy is the Lamb who was slaughtered--- to receive power and riches and wisdom and strength and honour and glory and blessing.*
>
> *Blessing and honour and glory and power belong to the one sitting on the throne and to the Lamb forever and ever.*
>
> *(Revelation 4: 8b; 11; 5: 9; 12; 13b).*

PRESENTATION BY THE REV. WILLIE NIXON[1]

This is a gripping and didactic short book which is primarily a testimony to the work of Christ in and around the life of Ken and Jeannie Scott. Ken, an Orcadian by birth, comes to faith in Christ at just 10 years old and powerfully writes: "I gave all that I knew of me to all that I knew of Christ"; it tells of a missionary call which began almost in tandem with his conversion to Christ and leads to an intriguing life journey which took him to Bible College, Costa Rica, Peru, Northern Ireland and to developing a growing intellectual and practical theology. Ken, clearly a conservative evangelical by background, opens a window for the reader into his personal experience of the Holy Spirit, in what I suspect to be a "mini-Pentecost" at a youth camp on the island of Hoy.

As he writes we discover the missionary insight which allows Ken to embrace a breadth of Christian traditions without prejudice or judgement. This book calls the reader to seek unity around the primary doctrines and encourages us not to allow the secondary issues to become divisive in God's Church. The book invites us to indulge in what amounts to being Ken's, almost creedal, personal thoughts on: giving, the Lord's Supper, the risk of the "personality cult" creeping into church leadership and the need for the centrality of the Cross and the Scriptures in the life of the Church. He achieves this without being overly heady or theological; this book is engaging because it is born of experience and comes from the heart.

In the pages of the book we find Ken gently using his lifetime as a Christian to teach, warn and encourage. There is a clear message that we need to be careful to seek conversion, but then to ensure we engage the heart of the great commission which is to "make disciples."

As the book comes to an end it is hard to miss that the word "missionary" and Dr Ken Scott are synonymous, with Ken giving his reader valuable wisdom and insight into what it means to be called and to go. In this short, easy read, we meet a man of integrity who is real about his own imperfections as a traveller on the road of faith in

---

[1] The Rev Willie Nixon and I have been acquainted for about six months and have discovered our mutual agreement on many matters of biblical faith and mission.

Jesus Christ and who reminds us all that we do not need a Damascus Road experience to accept the call of God into mission.

This book is well worth a read and is much more than a biography. It is full of advice given with the grace and wisdom of someone who has journeyed with Christ in His mission field for a lifetime.

Rev. Willie Nixon

Rector of Drumbeg Parish Church

PRESENTATION BY PASTOR ALAN BAIRD[2]

In presenting a book, an insight into the author is always helpful, as it gives an authenticity to the writing and therefore a greater incentive to engage with the contents.

The first time I met Ken Scott was in Peru in 2001 when he literally gave me, a stranger, "the shirt off his back". (The airline had lost our luggage.) That, I was to discover, was typical of the man. In the years since I have had the privilege of being a fellow traveller on his journey. I have travelled with, lived with, worked with, and shared the culture and passion for the people in the land of Peru and in the Irish Baptist College for some eight years. Those experiences have given me insight into a man of the very highest integrity and greatest generosity in thought and action that at times has left me speechless and humbled. I have seen in Ken Scott a man who has clearly experienced God at work in his life and who lives out his theology with no thought of the personal cost. I am privileged to call him my friend. It is this insight that enables me to unreservedly recommend this book.

This is a fascinating book that takes us on one man's journey, both physical and spiritual, from Orkney, a group of islands off the north coast of Scotland, to Peru a country on the west coast of South America. In that journey we see how God shaped Ken and Jeannie's lives and thinking.

The book is not intended to be deeply theological but in a very readable style we see how the combination of study, training, and missionary experience all combine to develop a true biblical grasp of important theological issues and their practical implementation. Here we see someone who has successfully combined study at the highest level with ministry at a practical level and not considered one to be inferior to the other. That the material is presented in a clear and gracious manner is the mark of a life shaped by God and impacted by a lifetime of service for God.

---

[2] Alan and I first met in Peru in the year 2001. We shared an office in the Irish Baptist College for two years, were fellow lecturers there for eight years, and travelled back and forth to Peru eight times together. We became and remain good friends. In our retirement we meet regularly for an Ulster fry!

Ken speaks to the importance of a biblical understanding of the great commission. i.e. it is not a matter of sharing the gospel, seeing conversions and planting churches. It is about "making disciples:" the training and equipping of those God has brought to faith. It includes implementing the principles of Acts 2, and James 2, of not ignoring practical needs. We also see the importance of a thorough understanding of the history and culture of those we seek to reach with the gospel and the problems caused by importing and implementing our own culture rather than applying biblical truths. He also addresses the importance of making judgement calls based on accurate objective information and the difference between leadership and control.

What makes this book a profitable read is that it is the experience of a lifetime spent at the coalface of mission rather than that of a spectator. This is a book that should have a wide appeal. Although clearly written from a missionary heart, there are principles that apply to all who seek to faithfully follow Christ wherever He has placed them. It is a privilege to present this book along with the prayer that God will be pleased to make it a help and blessing to many.

Pastor Alan Baird

Baptist pastor for over 25 years; full time lecturer on Practical Theology in the Irish Baptist College for several years; three times President of the Association of Baptist Churches in Ireland.

FOREWORD

My grandfather, Robert Eunson, on my mother's side, lived most of his life on the Island of Westray in Orkney. I remember him as a larger than life character who frequently spoke his mind. The last time I saw him alive was just before I left Orkney in early 1973, headed for Latin America. He reminisced more about his life than usual. For years he had emphasised, as Orcadians used to do, with a certain pride, the ageing process by claiming an extra year. He would say something like, "I am eighty years of age comes next year." Grandfather Eunson had served in the First World War as a groom, with the task of looking after horses. As a soldier he manned a machinegun. Like many others from that era he never spoke of whether he had killed men as he strafed enemy locations with bullets.

He was wounded twice. Once he was gassed and as a result was hospitalized and again when he was wounded on the thigh by a bullet. For some reason, on that, my final visit, he felt compelled to show me the wounds. He remembered that rations in the trenches were sparse for conscripted soldiers. "Some days just a piece of bread and tea made by boiling water from around your feet", he explained. The great thing about going to the hospital, he told me, with a twinkle in his eye, was that he gained weight. He had ended up just "like skin and bone and was down to ten stones and eight pounds." I remembered him always as a large big-boned Viking[3]. He continued:

> The time I was gassed, the damage to me was just on my legs, and they stuck together. The man in the next bed had suffered stomach damage from the gas. He could not eat, even if he had wanted to, so he offered his food to me. I was eating for two and gained three stones in weight in just a few weeks, before they sent me back to the trenches.

He told me the same story that several in my extended family will remember. He related the fact that one day while tending his horse, he heard a voice telling him to move to the other side. No sooner had he done so than the horse was shot dead by a German bullet at the very place where he had been standing. He was a man of faith in God and always believed the Lord had given the warning and saved his

---

[3] "Eunson" is a surname of Norwegian origin.

life. If he had died on that battlefield I, and several hundred Orcadians, spread over succeeding generations, would never have been born.

President Theodore Roosevelt reputedly said: "Old age is like everything else. To make a success of it, you've got to start young." That is precisely where I wish to begin in this short book. My mother, Catherine Eunson, daughter of Robert Eunson, a hard-working manual worker, was to marry John Adams Scott, a landowner. I was born Orcadian, the fourth son of eight siblings[4] from that union. What follows is an examination of how my own basic assumptions about life and living, formed from an Orcadian beginning, were later challenged, and modified.

As we get older, our immune system is not quite as robust, so we are more susceptible to coughs and colds. This fact, at the time of writing, is poignant in the light of the Coronavirus and its threat to septuagenarians. Being older I am more confident to tell my thoughts. Of course, not all may choose to read or listen. Hopefully, with age greater humility has come. It is easier to see something from another's point of view and it is good not to judge or criticize as much. Just as we all made, and make, many mistakes, we allow others to do the same. Possessions and status symbols become less important. In fact, as I get older, I am thankful for being *able* to grow old. Not everyone does and it seems that too many are dying before their time. With age comes gratitude and the knowledge that with every passing day we are blessed to be alive.

I have had some years to reflect on an often-quoted Bible verse. Romans 8:28 states: "And we know that in all things God works for the good of those who love him, who have been called according to his purpose." The verse was sent by Paul, in the first instance, to Christians in Rome facing persecution. This verse should not be used to reflect retrospectively and to explain that everything will become clear with hindsight. Paul did not promise the Christians in Rome that all the things that happened and were about to happen ("trouble or hardship or persecution or famine or nakedness or danger or sword" - 8:35), were good. Everything that happens is not good. This

---

[4] The eight siblings from the Scott family are: Thomas Mowat, Robert Eunson, Ivan Rendall, Kenneth David (me), Doreen Bertha, James Martin, George Reid, and Alistair Drever.

verse is not a promise that God will protect us from all harm and heartache. Therefore, not all that happens is the will of God. Nevertheless God, in His providence would then, and now, bring about His eternal purposes, and that is good.

Missionary service changed me, and I am certainly part of all that I met. In our multicultural world, we now find people of other cultures in almost every large city enclave. My own cross-cultural experiences as a lifetime missionary fills me with joy as I reflect. God brought about His purposes as I followed Jesus to what was for me, the ends of the earth. I discovered that He had already gone ahead long before I went. It was only far away until I went there.

Many different definitions are given to the word missionary. Some of them have been extremely general and others quite specific. In some circles the idea has been floated around that one is either a missionary or a mission field. This idea is that you either need to tell other people about Christ or that you need someone to tell you about Him. Other people think that anyone who receives financial support from individuals and/or churches, to be involved in Christian activity, is a missionary. Others see the word as only describing those involved in pioneer, cross-cultural, church planting work, because that is what they understand Paul to have been involved in. Obviously, not all such definitions can be correct.

People often ask me how they can know what God wants them to do? How can they know where God wants them to serve? Some people seem to be looking for some dramatic event in which God specifically tells them where God wants them to go or what He wants them to do.

Just as these are difficult questions to answer so too, I have discovered, is the exercise of studying a religion, not one's own. I have long-since argued in my writings in Spanish that evangelical Christians should be in the forefront of using a research-methodology that seeks to be objective in its approach. Expressed simply, the Christian investigator of another religion is required to "suspend judgement" and place his/her own faith "in parenthesis" until "creative interpretations" may be drawn.

Suffice to record, at this juncture, that for some it is important to know more about what it means to be a Baptist, Catholic, Lutheran,

Mennonite, Evangelical, or Charismatic, than what it means to be a simple, born-of-the-Spirit child of God. This occurs when we know more about our church tradition, denominational distinctives, governing statutes, or church service preferences than we know about the Word of God. Christianity has always been about introducing people to Jesus Christ, the one true path to God. Being in "this denomination" is not more important than being filled with the Spirit, being simple servants of the living God.

I invite you to accompany me on my own spiritual journey and to experience more of what the Apostle Paul wrote from prison in what transpired to be one of his last recorded letters:

> *When God our Saviour revealed his kindness and love, he saved us, not because of the righteous things we had done, but because of his mercy. He washed away our sins, giving us a new birth and new life through the Holy Spirit. He generously poured out the Spirit upon us through Jesus Christ our Saviour. Because of his grace he declared us righteous and gave us confidence that we will inherit eternal life* (Titus 3:4-8).

INTRODUCTION

It was in early October of 1968 that I sat down, somewhat tentatively, for my first introductory lecture, designed for new students in the Birmingham Bible Institute (BBI)[5]. I was still reeling from having bumped into Ron[6] in the corridor outside. He was a returning student and I had met him when I first came for my interview four months previously. He had told me then that the Lord had "entirely sanctified" him! I had puzzled over that ever since.

Before that had occurred, I was still contemplating the conversation I had with an itinerant Brethren evangelist I had met on the train, the previous evening, on my way down from Scotland. His comment that "Bible Colleges are nowhere found in Scripture" was still bothering me that morning. Then when Ron, mentioned above, asked me how far I had to travel from Orkney to buy my new checked corduroy jacket, I knew that I did not possess that kind of inner holiness he claimed! Life seemed a little confusing at that moment in time.

As I sat there, I cast my mind back to my spiritual journey thus far. I could never remember a time I did not believe in God or in Jesus Christ, God's Son. I recalled that at ten years of age my spiritual journey began when I gave all that I knew of me to all that I knew of Christ. I was convinced then that I was a sinner and that I needed Christ to be my Saviour. Since then I understood that, but for God's mercy and grace, I would not and could not know God.

I felt the "call"[7] of God on my life to be a missionary soon after my conversion to Christ. A missionary named Bill Speed, of the Evangelical Union of South America (EUSA), spoke in the recently formed Baptist Church in Kirkwall, Orkney (my parents were among the founding members in 1959), of his missionary work in Peru. I

---

[5] The Birmingham Bible Institute (BBI), Edgbaston, Birmingham, was an evangelical, interdenominational college designed to train students for Christian ministry, either at home or overseas. The institution comprised of several old Victorian style houses, located in a quiet part of the city. As in the case of several other Bible Colleges in the UK, BBI ceased to exist since then.

[6] Identity withheld.

[7] I will discuss my take on the concept of a "call" to a specific "life ministry" later in this short book.

was hooked and from that moment did not vacillate in believing that God had spoken to my heart. I was bound for Peru where I would be a missionary.

A life crisis came when I was fifteen and I contemplated leaving school. Indeed, my intent was to follow in the footsteps of two older brothers (Robert and Ivan) and become a farmer. As much as I enjoyed farm work that Summer, I had no peace until I decided, before the end of the holidays, to return to Stromness Academy for the two more years needed to complete my Higher Grades.

Two happy years followed my studies (1966-1968) when I did work alongside my father and two brothers on the large family farm. My two older brothers, mentioned above, were born farmers with a great eye for quality cattle and sheep, and pedigree animal breeding. I just enjoyed working. I owe it to my father's example of work that I should not ask anyone else to do what I was not prepared to do myself. This I would later take to Peru with me when I went as a young and very green missionary.

As I sought to grow spiritually my conviction increased that it was biblical to ask God to fill me with His Spirit. I believe God did just that, for the first time, one day when I was praying while tending the sheep alone. It became part of my prayer life to continue to ask God to give me more of His Spirit. During that time the Rev Kenneth McNeish, the pastor of Kirkwall Baptist Church, encouraged me on my journey into Bible College. Some in my home church had hoped I would apply to the Bible Training Institute in Glasgow. After all, Birmingham was "too far doon Sooth. It was in England!"

My thoughts were interrupted when the Rev Stanley Jebb entered to give his lecture on "dangers in the ministry." I thought I had already encountered some dangers, within the last 24 hours, and was wondering what I was doing there! With notebook in hand I was ready to write. Sadly, I no longer have a copy of the lecture notes in my archive but remember, as if yesterday, the three main dangers outlined.

Pride was mentioned as an attitude that would bring a Christian ministry to ruin. It was not difficult to assent to that in my mind. My parents had often railed against braggarts. Of course, I knew that pride was more insidious than just blowing one's own trumpet[8]. The misuse of, or misappropriation of, or a desire for money and wealth[9], was presented as the second danger to ministry. My father had always exemplified to me what integrity should be, down to the last penny, and I struggled with the idea that a Christian could be dishonest with money. When Stanley Jebb proceeded to explain that inappropriate sexual behaviour was the third major cause of damage to a Christian leader's testimony, I was incredulous[10]. My family and church upbringing left me in no doubt that any, and all, sexual activity was to be restricted within marriage. That was non-negotiable[11]. I have never forgotten that lecture. I will pick up on these themes later in this short book.

At nineteen years of age I was the youngest among a student body of over 100. All were enrolled with a view to training for Christian ministry, either at home or overseas. At that time Bible Colleges did not like to accept students straight from school. My rather sheltered Orcadian upbringing was exposed to a multicultural city. Besides, College life each day was regimented by house prayers at 6.30 am, followed by personal devotions, chores, breakfast, classes, lunch,

---

[8] Scripture came to mind: Isaiah 66:2b: "I will bless those who have humble and contrite hearts, who tremble at my word." Micah 6:8: "No, O people, the Lord has told you what is good, and this is what he requires of you: to do what is right, to love mercy, and to walk humbly with your God." Isaiah 66:2b: "I will bless those who have humble and contrite hearts, who tremble at my word."

[9] Scripture certainly warned against this: Psalm 62:10b, "And if wealth increases, don't make it the centre of your life…" and 1 Timothy 6:9-10, "Those who want to get rich fall into temptation and a snare and many foolish and harmful desires which plunge men into ruin and destruction. For the love of money is a root of all sorts of evil, and some by longing for it have wandered away from the faith and pierced themselves with many griefs."

[10] I confess that I probably had the same battles that any adolescent young man might have had. Nevertheless, there was, and is, a clear distinction between appropriate and inappropriate behaviour with a person of the opposite sex. While in Stromness Academy, completing my secondary education, I usually did not believe the boasts of sexual conquests from my classmates. In retrospect I know that I was naïve. Two guiding verses of Scripture for me were: Psalm 119:11, "I have hidden your word in my heart; that I might not sin against you" and Psalm 119:105, "Your word is a lamp to guide my feet and a light for my path."

[11] I considered my girlfriend back in Orkney to be the bonniest lass I had ever seen, and a fine Christian, but my major concern was whether she would agree to life as a missionary in Peru!

some more classes, and controlled study between 6.30-9.30 pm. Lights had to be out by 10.30 pm. I enjoyed the studies and activities, and my faith was underpinned by what I learned.

A sizeable group of students adhered to a version of John Wesley's teaching on entire sanctification. Ron, mentioned above, was one day claiming he had not sinned "for two months" when George[12], a down to earth Northern Irishman, instantly kicked him on the shin. Ron responded with a punch to George's chest. George quietly responded: "well you have now!"

BBI was also going through quite a pronounced Pentecostal phase. I remember several memorable experiences of preaching where people responded to sermons and came to Christ. More than once I recall the need to "enable" people to receive Christ. Others call this "deliverance", but I prefer to share the events carefully. Silly things happen in the name of Christ and are claimed to be from the Spirit. For instance, I was sad when, in my last year of studies, my girlfriend and I decided we were not for each other. In the wake of that event, a fellow student named Steve[13], uttered a "prophecy" that I should marry another student called Mary[14]. I replied, "I do not think so." His challenge was: "Are you going against God?" "No, you great clonk," I replied, "I am going against you." That was one of several such experiences. I trace my dislike of Christians "playing God" by declaring invasive so-called "words from God."

I do not deny that I passed through various experiences of the Holy Spirit at that time, that changed, and continue to change my life, and I believe it to be necessary to trust in the action of the Holy Spirit always and in everything. Besides, various members of my family are part of the so-called charismatic movement. I have never considered myself to be Pentecostal although I hold Pentecostals in great respect as belonging to the family of God in Christ.

I learned that classical Pentecostal doctrine included what they called "the full gospel", a foursquare message, that "Christ saves, heals,

---

[12] Identity withheld.

[13] Identity withheld. "Steve" was an Anglican charismatic who later married, had a family, and became a missionary in Lima, Peru.

[14] Identity withheld

18

baptises in the Spirit and is coming again." Other sectors of the Pentecostals added to their foursquare message, by declaring that Christ "sanctifies." This was a reminder that John Wesley's teaching on holiness from the nineteenth century was another antecedent. Three distinguishable forms of Pentecostalism were becoming evident on the global stage, even then. They are now the "Classical Pentecostals" (as above), the "movement of charismatic renewal" and the "independent new churches" that are similar in doctrine to Pentecostals. There are many Catholic Charismatics in the second category.

It was a surprise to me to learn that the Pentecostals I came to know were Christian in their affirmation of the cardinal doctrines of Christianity. I had been led to expect them to believe that unless a person "spoke in tongues" he/she was "not saved." I discovered they, like all Christians, adhered to the biblical doctrines of the Trinity, Christ's Incarnation, the Atonement through Christ's death and resurrection, the need for faith in Jesus Christ in order to be saved, the presence and power of the Divine Holy Spirit in every authentic believer and the blessed hope that Christ will return in order to consummate the Kingdom of God.

When free from studies and preaching commitments, I would visit Selly Oak Elim Church and loved Pastor Capel's succinct Gospel preaching (usually no more than fifteen minutes) and the resulting response. During my last year at BBI, I regularly chose Graham Street Elim Church, where in practically every sermon Pastor Coles exuded his pastoral ministry. I invariably came away blessed, encouraged in my faith and in my relationship to Christ. There is no doubt in my mind that it was while at BBI that I had developed an interdenominational ethos in my approach to fellowship.

During the Summer after graduation I was "employed" (not for the first time) by BBI as a handyman, led a children's campaign in an Elim Church and a youth Camp from a Brethren Assembly in Birmingham, near to Snowdonia in Wales, where a number of young people came to Christ. I was again confronted by the need to pray, along with elder Roy Fellows (a schoolteacher) from a Brethren Assembly in Birmingham, and ask the Lord to rebuke demonic activity in the life of one young man who had been paralysed by fear, after dabbling in the occult. The Lord set him free! Those were all experiences that formed me theologically and helped me appreciate the rich diversity in the Church.

It was in July of 1971 that I also visited Northern Ireland for the first time. There was much unrest at that time, and I witnessed the military presence in Belfast. Besides preaching on the streets, I took part in a march on July the 12th! I was invited to hear Dr Ian Paisley preach in his church on Sunday. I admit I was in awe of his physical presence and style as he entered the pulpit. In fact, I remember his text and its delivery – "The flesh profiteth nothing" - but could not for the life of me understand how in his sermon he interpreted this to mean "the outward trappings of the Catholic Church." Nor did I appreciate how he developed his theme from the text to make the assertion that "they (the Catholics) believe you receive grace through your stomach." I understood this to be a reference to the Mass but have never been convinced that the pulpit should be used to attack something that is sacred to so many[15].

I owe it to my parents for teaching me, by example, that the basis for fellowship was not denominational, but on profession of faith in Jesus Christ. Before my parents were part of the new Baptist Church in Kirkwall in 1959, we had been taken faithfully as children to the Dounby United Free (UF) Church of Scotland. Our family doctor, Dr Emslie, was, at that time, their acting pastor. On returning to Orkney, several friends from BBI and I led an outreach campaign in the Dounby UF Church. Afterwards, I was asked to be their pastor. So it was that I sought to serve the Dounby UF Church for the following year and a half. As a non-ordained pastor and as a Baptist I was content to allow an ordained UF minister (either from Shetland or Scotland) to lead the sacraments.

I came to know and appreciate Jim Stockan, who attended the Dounby UF Church. He was a godly Christian businessman who made oatcakes. I still buy them – they are the best! I am sure that many visits to his house, which always ended in prayer, were probably insensitive intrusions of a young man. Jim's godly wife May was always welcoming. Jim had a way of repeating things! For instance, I learned, and cannot forget, that "the glory must always be for the Lord because the Lord does not share His glory." I also

---

[15] I believed by then, as now, that many Roman Catholics have as real a faith in Jesus Christ as many "evangelicals."

remember him often repeating: "Ken, if you are ever accused and are guilty, hands up to the Lord. If you are not guilty as accused, hands up to the Lord!" How could I forget that? I have had to practise both approaches many times!

During my time back in Orkney, I arranged for a visit in 1972 of my good Welsh friend Alan Penduck. Along with young folk from Dounby and the Kirkwall Baptist Church, we went to the Youth Hostel on the island of Hoy for a Christian Camp. It was there that one night, after our devotional session, the older young people, some leaders, Alan, and I met for prayer. I remember I decided that instead of just listening to Alan's talks it would be good to ask God to meet us and bless us.

What followed left me as a spectator! From the first moment God moved and, although folk asked me to pray with/for them, I knew and still know, that God was moving by His Spirit. I remember my younger brother Martin's prayer for God to bless. Jim Stockan's daughter Anne immediately followed in clear praise to God. Others started to worship the Lord spontaneously and we all continued well into the morning. Some had so used their voices that they were hoarse! Alan and I finally took a stroll in the moonlight before dawn to contemplate what I believe to this day was a mighty mini movement of God. Several of those present that night later went into Christian ministry, including both mentioned above. I certainly gave and give God the glory for what He did. I know I did not do it! Aye, the glory was His.

PRELIMINARY REFLECTIONS

Two fellow students at BBI, Chris Papworth and May Walker, both preceded me to Peru. They joined the Regions Beyond Missionary Union (RBMU – later part of Latin Link), an interdenominational evangelical faith mission. I was persuaded to make application to the same organization. By that stage I believed, at least in my head, that everything, absolutely everything, had to do with God[16]. Thus, everything was ultimately for God's glory. Furthermore, Christ had declared about His own divine "call": "The Son of Man came not to be served, but to serve, and to give his life as a ransom for many…" (Matthew 20:28). As illustrated above, I knew I was on a journey and

---

[16] The Apostle Paul wrote: "All things are from him and to him" (Romans 11:36).

that I had much yet to learn about service to God. Although I believed that I was being led by the Lord, I would learn little by little that God would direct my steps[17].

CHAPTER ONE
OTHER CULTURES

One of the joys in my life has not only been the privilege of reading about other cultures but of experiencing them. On an academic level I was instructed to be value free in my judgements, but the years have taught me that in each culture, including my own, there are positive, negative, and neutral elements. The first lesson is simply to acknowledge difference. While my theology often led me to recoil, social anthropologists opened my mind to appreciate rich variations. However, nothing quite equalled first-hand experience. A few examples will illustrate what I mean.

My arrival in Costa Rica, on the 1st May 1973, was at night. It took a while for my mind to settle down that night in the humid heat of Curridabat, a suburb of San José, Costa Rica, to the new sound of crickets. My Latin American experience had begun. I hastily downed my breakfast the next morning of fresh, crusty bread, a boiled egg and freshly made filter coffee with hot milk. The head of the Castro family, where full board had been arranged for me, was a coffee taster. For the next year I looked forward to that breakfast and a love affair with good filter coffee began.

My Spanish language studies commenced and on that first morning on route to classes I learned that space took on a new meaning. I travelled to and from *El Instituto de Lengua Española* squeezed onto a bus, then back for a lunch in my Costa Rican "home" for the national staple of rice and beans. This was usually accompanied by either a pork chop or some other protein. There were new tastes and I liked them, although I was to learn that others did not always appreciate the inclusion of garlic in the dishes I had eaten! For my mother, brought up as she was, in relative poverty, to exceed half an onion in a meal for everyone, would have been extravagance! Nevertheless, Latin American cuisine, and my appreciation of its many dishes, had started.

It is always dangerous to oversimplify when it comes to generalizations as one country differs from another. Nevertheless, I did discover certain Latin features that were to carry over into Peru. One of those relates to time keeping. It was common for people to arrive late. Whereas my arrival for classes required me to be punctual

– of course the language school was run by Americans – this did not hold when it came to other occasions. The notable exception to this would be a funeral! Death waits for no one! Years later, while in Lima, Jeannie and I had invited our good friend Jacob Huamán to breakfast. That proved to be an extreme case of lateness. He finally arrived after midday with the words, "I got lost a little." Och, Lima was big and that was all he needed to say. We shared lunch with him.

When it came to Latins, I think I learned to lay aside, what is an ongoing area of tension for westerners, by knowing that I needed to arrive five minutes late. It was a start. Nevertheless, when it came to missionary colleagues, or when back "home" in the West, I never learned to be late. I was back in Peru in 2019 and met up with Alicia, who had worked alongside me in Tacna, Peru as Mission Administrator, by then married to a lawyer from the Dominican Republic. She was stranded in Lima due to visa issues, with her two eleven years old twin daughters. We, all four, arranged to meet for lunch at 1.00 pm in Larco Mar, Lima in a small restaurant. I had mentally planned that I would be free and in my favourite bookshop, *El Virrey* in Miraflores, by 3.00 pm, at the latest. It was 4.30 pm when I hailed their taxi and said goodbye. Alicia was in no mood to just "grab" lunch, as we do, but she needed to catch up and just chat. Table talk is part of the meal. In later years when I did mission networking in Lima, I would arrange to meet my Peruvian friends and colleagues in the *Haití Café* in Miraflores. Indeed, when in Lima by myself, I often went there for my American breakfast or just for a *café con leche* (or two or three!), and then my own "after time." Pure joy!

Before I move on, I should mention that Costa Rica will always hold a special part in my heart because it was there that I met Jeannie. While my departure to Costa Rica for Spanish language study was delayed by several months, on the other side of the Atlantic, Jeannie Yoder`s departure from Delaware to Costa Rica was accelerated by several months. In God`s providence we were to meet for the first time on a bus in San José in October of 1973 [18]. Our romance developed from there.

It was in February 1974 that Jeannie was told that her father, then 68 years of age, was dying of cancer. He had been operated on 13 years

---

[18] I have told this story in *Life Stories of an Unworthy Servant,* 2020, 14-16.

before and had had his stomach removed. By then Jeannie and I were in love and she asked me to accompany her to her home in Delaware in the USA for the funeral. Nothing prepared me for the world I was about to enter. We left Costa Rica together for her Dad`s funeral on the 18th February 1974.

Jeannie and I were picked up at the airport by her nephew Ronnie and her brother Doyle, who, with his six-foot four-inch frame promptly "fell on my neck and kissed me." Aaaahhhh! We were driven directly to the "viewing", before which Jeannie had put up her hair and had taken out her "head covering." Jeannie belonged to the Mennonite denomination, and women did not cut their hair and it was a practice to gather it up and wear a covering. After meeting Jeannie's oldest brother Samuel (in a grey sports jacket with an open necked shirt) and his wife Effie, I was immediately aware of men in plain black suits and in what appeared to me to be clerical collars. After a query from me about all the "clergy" present Jeannie clarified that many stricter Mennonite men dressed that way.

Thereafter, I was on a steep cultural learning curve as I met siblings, their spouses and extended family and the Mennonite community at the funeral. I attended Greenwood Mennonite Church on Sunday along with Jeannie. As we lined up to enter, I became aware of the men greeting Bishop John Mishler with a kiss on the lips. I immediately asked Jeannie what that was. She replied: "Ah, that is the holy kiss", to which I remember that I replied, "There is nothing holy about that!" I made sure my right hand was extended and my left clenched when I greeted Bishop John! Bishop John Mishler was to perform our wedding ceremony in the same church (the first of a non-Mennonite to marry "in") on the 28th December 1974.

New cultural experiences were evident at every turn. It is too complicated to include the differences already encountered by an Orcadian in the many variations experienced of Scottish, English, and American cultural idiosyncrasies. When Jeannie and I travelled together to Peru, as a recently married couple, on the 1st March 1975 we had plenty cultural adjustments awaiting us as we began to "know" each other. Jeannie's account[19], written elsewhere, of her cultural transition to Peru, is good reading.

My purpose here is to concentrate on Peru and how my life has been enriched as a result. I would suggest that most, if not all, missionaries experience "culture shock". It becomes evident when we ex-pats speak among ourselves. There are only two, or perhaps, if I am honest, three (maybe four!) missionaries who were so negative about Peru that I could hardly listen to them. One missionary, not one of the negative ones, told me within five minutes of meeting him: "Do not trust any Peruvian!" When I challenged him by replying, "but you are married to a Peruvian." He simply retorted: "That is why I am telling you so." As time went on, I came to understand him. I discovered that he loved his wife dearly and everything Peruvian, especially the food. Life is fascinating, is it not?

Culture shock is inevitable and leads, if unresolved, to fatigue. Fatigue, in turn, leads to negativity and discouragement. Our cultural understanding is what determines more of our behaviour than we wish to admit. The "what" of my responses is explained by the "why" of my motives. A little understanding in this area enables us to develop good interpersonal relationships. Of course, as my good missionary colleague indicated, as the melancholic that he is, trust is at the centre of relationships. I soon learned that prices were not always as they appeared, whether when buying vegetables in the market or bartering over a taxi fare. Our western reaction was that we were being lied to or worse still, being "cheated." That did not feel good to me, but Peruvians were just attempting to make a day's wage. Peruvians inherently understand that world. How many times did I not wait in vain for folk to turn up "when they said they would" or to pay me back when they had "borrowed" from me?

In my next chapter I will indicate briefly how the Spanish arrived in Peru in the sixteenth century as "friends" and were received as such. The Spanish Conquest that ensued could only be described as "treachery". Indeed, even with the passage of five centuries, the indigenous population never regained trust in the "Conquistadors." We have our own way of explaining this: "once bitten, twice shy." I was to learn that trust works two ways. In the West, at the risk of

---

[19] See *Life Stories of an Unworthy Servant,* 2020, 24-26, for Jeannie's take on our first few years in Peru.

generalisations, we "are innocent until proven guilty", so we do not warm to the idea that we might be "guilty until proven innocent." My mentor's words: "Ken, when you are accused, and are innocent, hands up to the Lord", came to my rescue many times. Of course, I have also been accused, when guilty! In that case, truth, repentance and, again, "hands up to the Lord" was the solution. In our twenty first century I have witnessed in Peru the ugliness of the internet being used (by Christians?) to make "false" accusations. That is why I have never joined Facebook.

I do have "friends" in Peru, and soon after arriving in Peru, I realized that some American colleagues understood better than their UK counterparts that "friends" in high places, and "recommendations", got things done. Two American missionaries come to mind. Their "ministries" had developed, over the years into that of enabling new missionaries to obtain their Peruvian documents more rapidly. It seemed to me that their confidence and brashness were strengths. I am not suggesting any impropriety, just their ability to adapt to the culture! By the way, soon after Jeannie and I arrived in Northern Ireland in 1991, I was stopped by a policeman for speeding on Sunday evening when driving home from church. According to his radar gun, I was "doing 47 miles per hour, and accelerating, in a 30 mile an hour speeding zone." I accepted the £20 penalty and paid it off within days. Fortunately for me, that was before penalty points were added to driving licences. When I related the experience to a company director in our church, he challenged me: "Why did you not tell me, I could have got you off?" Aye, that really happened! I was never comfortable with that, either in Peru or in the UK. It was not "what" one knew, but "who" one knew.

Perhaps my Northern Irish colleagues understood better than I did the trusted status of the one who recommends another. A friend of a friend in high office carries weight because he is trustworthy. Is that not how it works? With such an introduction, one is "in." Loyalty in every culture is based primarily on trust. Wherever I travelled in Peru, "favours" were called in or obtained, based on friendship. I witnessed this at all levels in Peru, especially as evangelicals became more involved in politics. In a country where "all roads lead to Lima" there were churches in Lima composed of believers who came from another region in Peru, who then drew in families from that area as they migrated to Lima.

It is one thing to defend friends, but families and their possessions are causes for which Peruvians would give everything. Our western concept of the "nuclear" family needs to take a back seat when seeking to understand how a respectable family operates in Peru. Family is all-important in Peru. There is the "inner" circle of the husband/wife, children, parents, grandparents, and there is the "outer" circle of uncles/aunts and first cousins. That closes the Peruvian family. For Peruvians, family is one thing and "friends" is another. No Peruvian is expected to make it on his/her own. They all work from the position of anticipated weakness. Age brings wisdom and respect. Friends are important but when the chips are down each person goes to his/her family.

Not long before Jeannie and I left Peru for ministry in the Belfast Bible College in Northern Ireland in 1991, a short-term worker, who will remain nameless, came to me to ask advice about "courting" a young lady he had met in the church he attended. The lady in question, had moved to Lima from Apurímac, was staying with her uncle and aunt in Lima and, according to him, was keen. My advice was simple. Given that they had already spoken, before proceeding any further with the relationship, he needed to chat it through with the uncle and aunt. I added that it would be wise thereafter, once permission was given, to meet only where they both could be seen, such as in the lounge.

A week had not passed when the young man came to me in a terrible state, because, as he explained, the uncle and aunt had prohibited him from meeting the young lady again. "What did you do to cause such a reaction?" I asked. "Nothing" he replied. He added that they were angry with him and called him "handyman." I had to insist on asking several times before he replied incredulously, "We only went behind the tree in the patio to kiss." "You great clonk" was my reply. "Why, what did I do wrong? I kissed all the other girls I went out with back home in England." Two weeks later he came back to me and apologised for his behaviour. Unfortunately, he then went on to ask about another young lady he had met and required my advice! I was out of there!

Cultures are different. There is no doubt in my mind about that. What about ethics? We British are heavy on articulating rules and responsibility. Rules are there to guide us into behaviour. Would it be true to suggest that Peruvians envisage rules similarly as guidelines

28

provided there is some personal benefit? One example is that we stop at traffic lights! This may have changed over the years in Peru, but if there is no traffic camera evident, and no pedestrians, or traffic, why stop? The same kind of logic may be applied to driving in Lima or when lining up in a queue.

A new English missionary had been on the Lima scene for about a year. In 1991 I asked him to accompany me at about 11.00 pm to travel to the centre of Lima. I was on an errand to pick up a medical doctor in the Mission and take him to the house of one of the single lady missionaries who had taken ill. Several blocks away from my destination I noticed the traffic lights just ahead had turned red. The car beside me started moving through the lights, as did I, as we both made sure there was no traffic crossing. The policeman, whom I had already noticed, decided to pull me over. The inevitable questions ensued. "Did you not see the red light?" "Yes, I did" I replied. "Do you know that is against the law?" "Yes, I do" was my confession. "Why then did you drive through?" My reply was honest: "I drove through because I was going to collect a doctor to take him to tend to a single lady missionary who is sick." The policeman's reply was polite: "O.K. off you go and drive carefully."

My colleague turned to me incredulously and said: "He let you go. At no time did you tell a lie. You simply told the truth. He let you off!" What I am about to relate now could not be invented. The same English colleague, who did not last in Lima, had suffered fifteen accidents, thus far, during his first year in the city. The accidents were minor, but the cost had built up. What was amazing was that he believed he was not at fault on any of the occasions. For instance, he related that the bus came over into his lane and clipped his front wing. "He moved into my lane!" I had come to understand that Lima traffic hates a vacuum. He failed to understand me when I stated: "Bus is big. Car is small. Car gives way." Reader make of that what you will!

It was Robert Burns who wrote: "O wad some Power the giftie gie us. To see oursels as ithers see us! It wad frae monie a blunder free us." [20] So how do Peruvians see us? I know of some Peruvian perspectives regarding us because they have been said to me or about

---

[20] James A. Mackay, Edited and Introduced, Second Edition, 1990, *The Complete Works of Robert Burns,* Ayr: Alloway Publishing, 182.

others. Thank you to true friends for speaking of what you see. Do we not come on strong? Are we not inflexible? We do not like tears/emotions – said to my wife Jeannie! Do we not tend to over-dominate? Do we have little tolerance with mistakes? Do we manipulate people? Are we demanding of others? Is our work/ministry our god? Do we give the impression that we know everything? Can we do everything better? Are we too independent?

Ah, but how do we see our Peruvian brothers and sisters in our moments of weakness? Why are you so disorganized? How do you forget obligations? Why do you not follow through? Why are you so undisciplined? Why are your priorities out of order? Why do you decide through feelings? Why do you look for credit? Why do you make excuses? Why dwell on the trivial? Why are you controlled by circumstances? Why are you so fickle and forgetful? Why do you seek to lead by decree? Why can there be no retraction when the rules are broken?

CONCLUSIONS

When we seek to communicate our faith in Christ and our personal commitment to Jesus Christ, we need to know how people from other cultures tick. It helps if this is mutual. How does a missionary tick? There are undoubtedly times when we fail to understand, the one the other. Psalm 15:1 declares: "Who may worship in your sanctuary, Lord? Who may enter your presence on your holy hill?" This is followed by a list of godly qualities such as "those who lead blameless lives and do what is right, speaking the truth from sincere hearts. Those who refuse to gossip or harm their neighbours or speak evil of their friends…." I have Peruvian friends, and although I may not be family in the sense of race – I am in Christ – a principle that guides me when I do not understand you, my friends, is found in v.4b "and [those who] keep their promises even when it hurts." Friends are friends forever, so I keep my promises to you and refuse to speak evil of you, even when it hurts me.

CHAPTER TWO
PERUVIAN CONTEXT

THE INCA EMPIRE[21]

The origin of the Empire of the Incas is shrouded in mystery; one myth speaks of the Sun god, who created a brother and his sister, Manco Capac y Mama Ocllo. They were placed on an island in Lake Titicaca and were given a golden staff, with the instruction that they should walk from there until they would be led to finally plant the staff in the earth at an ideal spot. This transpired finally when Manco Capac thrust the staff into the ground in what is today the city of Cuzco (meaning "navel of the earth" in Quechua) which soon became the centre of the Inca Empire, el *Tawantinsuyo*, with its four regions (*suyos*). From Cuzco the Empire spread through the Andes mountains on the western part of South America, as far north to what is today the south of Colombia, and in the south to the central valley of Chile.

From the thirteenth century, under the leadership of successive Incas, other civilizations were conquered, until at last, in the fifteenth and sixteenth centuries, the empire grew to its maximum extent, although some territories were never finally subjugated. Each *ayllu* (family), or agrarian group made up of extended families, based on el *ayni* (reciprocity), owned and cultivated their lands within their own communal territory. Decisions about land use and on other matters relating to welfare of the community were taken by the head of the *ayllu*, the *curaca,* who, before deciding, would also consult the other main leaders.

The Incas demanded absolute submission, from those conquered, to the leading officials of the Empire and, through them, to the Emperor, the Inca. Those who rebelled were cruelly punished and rebellious populations were re-established with the agreement of other groups that had proven their loyalty. When deemed to be possible, the governors attempted to rule through local *curacas,* and the ideal was to incorporate them within the official local Inca hierarchy. The continuity of the practice of local pre-existing

---

[21] See Kenneth D. Scott Eunson, 2016, *Nuevos Movimientos Religiosos. Un acercamiento interdisciplinaro.* Tomo I, Lima, Ediciones Puma, pp. 57-58.

traditions was permitted, under the condition that the supremacy of the Inca cult be recognized.

In the year 1525 there was an abrupt rupture of what was until then an orderly succession of governors. Two of the Inca's sons: Huascar, born of his principle wife, and Atahualpa, born of a concubine, held to their rights to the throne. After some five years of war, Atahualpa came out victorious. He captured and executed Huascar and assumed control of the empire, which was still in a state of recuperation when the Spanish Conquistadors arrived.

THE SPANISH CONQUEST

A combination of luck, resolute avarice and ingenuity permitted the Conquistador Francisco Pizarro and his band of 168 Spaniards, to conquer the Inca Empire. The first generation of Chroniclers (Guaman Poma de Ayala, Cieza de León y Garcilaso de la Vega and others) were fascinated by the history. The blind lawyer William H. Prescott wrote his *History of the Conquest of Peru* in 1847 from those and other informants without having visited Peru. Even now no one has written a better book about this period of Peruvian history than the historian John Hemming, whose *The Conquest of the Incas* has become so magisterial that it must not be missed. The capture of Atahualpa in the Andean city of Cajamarca by Pizarro caused the fall of the empire.

Francisco Pizarro arrived in Cajamarca, Perú, in November of 1532, with 168 men and 62 horses: the conquest was sealed within the next few hours. After reading the *Requerimiento* (Requirement) [22] to Atahualpa, who threw down "The Word of God" that was offered to him. Pizarro's men, with shouts of "Saint James", fell on the Inca and his followers in the central square of Cajamarca. Without delay, Atahualpa's subjects delivered the ransom of gold and silver that the Spaniards requested for his release. However, despite fulfilling Pizarro's request, Atahualpa was sentenced to death, for having assassinated his brother Huascar.

---

[22] The Requirement was a document that included Christian doctrine, eulogised the Pope and the King, while inviting the conquered nation to swear allegiance to the king of Spain, while also permitting the gospel to be preached within its territories.

The plan was to execute the Inca leader at the stake on the 29th of August 1533, but at the last moment he agreed to be baptized as a Christian and die by garrotte. The imperial belief that dominated Atahualpa's thinking would have left him no difficulty in choosing strangulation as opposed to being burned. His ideology dictated that if he had died at the stake, he would have been denied the possibility of his body entering the next world. They still burned his body!

The "Christian" faith was accepted, in the first instance, given the supposed superiority of the Christian deities over the "divine" Inca. Nevertheless, this should not eclipse what the indigenous population suffered through the destruction of their society, the demographic catastrophe, the challenge of Christianity to local religion and the transfer of the Andean population into an "inferior caste." Scholars agree regarding the psychological shock caused by the impact of having suffered such a serious defeat at the hands of the Spaniards.

The religion of the Inca nobility was denied to the masses, although the divinity of the supreme leader was acknowledged by the population. The subjects of the Inca Empire retained their sacred places (*huacas*). After the Conquest, the first Inca practice to disappear was that of giving homage to the sun. The gods of local communities were adored in parallel to the religion of Inca nobility. Across the centuries the rural communities continued to pay homage to the *huacas* and synthesised this with the new Christian faith.

Forced labour was imposed on the indigenous population, that is, on a people who before then had carried out their own rites when they celebrated festivals and religious ceremonies as they worked in community. Distilled alcohol, previously kept only for their religious festivals, became available for all on a level without precedent. In the same way coca leaves (a powerful stimulant that reduced their hunger, thirst and the pain suffered from their hard work) which was used under the Inca's control by the elite in religious ceremonies or to barter, was made available on a new level. So it was that alcohol and coca leaves (elements previously dedicated solely to Inca rituals) enabled the control of those forced to work, while at the same time encouraging a revival of the veneration given to their local *huacas*. This also enabled an idealization of the Inca past.

TWENTIETH CENTURY

A hundred years ago the Roman Catholic Church was so dominant in Peru that its presence represented a religious monopoly. Only 1.5 percent of the population belonged to Christian non-Catholic churches. In 1900, all the non-Catholic Christians, who were called "evangelicals", were Protestants. The other 5 percent of the population declared themselves to be not religious or affiliated to a non-Christian religious group.

Historically, all Peruvian culture was Catholic to the very smallest detail. Everyone was born Peruvian and Catholic. People saw the world through Catholic eyes and the non-Catholic citizens were, in some sense, people without an identity. After Peruvian independence from Spain in the twentieth century, a certain legal separation between the Roman Catholic Church and the State occurred, but even then, the Catholic Church still functioned as if it held a regional religious monopoly.

A fundamental change began to take place about the middle of the twentieth century. From that time the same religious Catholic monopoly did not exist to the same degree, but rather pluralistic religious expressions became a feature of society. There was a developing gap between natality and sacramentality. The driving force behind that change during the ultimate four or five decades has been the phenomenal growth of the Charismatic Pentecostal movement.

On the other hand, it is worth clarifying that it is difficult to speak of atheism or secularization in Peru much as one does when referring to Europe, primarily because the Latin continent continues to be eminently religious by nature. In Peru one breathes religiosity. All the signs point in that direction: the quantity of churches and evidence of religious practices. José Luis Pérez Guadalupe argues that it is a matter "not of religious demand, but of the ecclesiastic on offer. That is, it is not that the people do not want to believe. The people want to believe. What is happening is that there are no missionary priests and there are no pastoral agents there to satisfy that religious need."

It was Pope John Paul II who proposed a "new evangelization" focussed on the "conversion" in a Catholic sense of a process, during a lifetime, of leaving sin and turning to Christ, instead of conversion understood in the Protestant sense or in the Pentecostal/Charismatic sense of an "event." To be Peruvian and to be Catholic is no longer synonymous. Given that the number of non-Catholics is growing, it has become socially acceptable to choose to be Evangelical and not Catholic.

The Roman Catholic Church began to compete for their members with both offensive and defensive diverse strategies. Of those, the one that has given the best results, is the charismatic renewal movement, in which large sectors of the Peruvian Catholic population participate. Defensively, Peruvian Catholics have used a variety of ways to put obstacles to limit the growth of non-Catholic religion. This includes pressure on the Government to approve laws that intend to restrict the activities of "religious sects" and of developing programmes designed so that Catholics do not give in to the proselytising of those groups.

Despite the Catholic response, Pentecostal/charismatic Christianity continues to grow. The growth of the Pentecostal/charismatic movement appears to be related also to the process of urbanization. Up to this date, the Catholic Church has not had much success in providing social and religious support in the shanty towns, while some of the Pentecostal/charismatic churches have had incredible "success" in these contexts. Instead of establishing churches "for the poor", these new churches were planting churches "of the poor." Besides, many of the same new church leaders were poor themselves, and this has made a great difference in leading to their growth.

Compared to the traditional Protestant churches, the Pentecostal/charismatic movement has had much more success in Peru. In many cases, this is due mainly to the fact, even when foreign missionaries have been present, that Peruvians have risen rapidly in their standing to positions of leadership. In their majority, these Pentecostal churches had less resources than the historic Protestant churches and less educational formation, but by the 1960s there were as many Pentecostal Christians in Peru as traditional Evangelicals.

Since approximately 1960, the Pentecostal/charismatic movement has grown rapidly and has produced an extensive swathe of Pentecostal and neo-Pentecostal denominations. Many of these churches support the "gospel and prosperity", with the promise of financial blessings for those who place their trust and limited resources in the work of their church. What separates many of them from other evangelicals, is their willingness to go where the people are: in the poor sectors of the cities, and in that way to become part of the neighbourhood. Their leaders are available to help and pray for the marginalised and for all who ask for support.

Pérez Guadalupe refers to the growth of evangelicals in Peru up to the year 2002[23], to represent some 3,415,000 members. Douglas Jacobsen[24], writing in 2011, presents a religious profile of Peru where some 90% of the population is "Christian". Of those, about 75% would be traditional Catholics, 7% Charismatic Catholics, 2% Protestant evangelicals and about 6% Pentecostal/charismatic. Pérez Guadalupe calculates that between 13 and 15% of Peruvians are evangelicals. According to him, about 69% of Peruvian evangelicals follow a Pentecostal line; about 24% are non-Pentecostals and the other 7% of evangelicals are neo-Pentecostals or charismatics. It is good that Pérez Guadalupe does not include the Mormons, the Jehovah Witnesses, the Seventh Day Adventists, or the Israelites of the New Universal Covenant[25] within his statistics when he calculates the total number of Peruvian evangelicals.

The Assemblies of God is now the largest Pentecostal church in Peru. Peruvian Pentecostalism began when Howard and Catherine Cragin, a North American couple, arrived in 1911. Soon afterwards others appeared, including the first Assemblies of God missionaries in 1922. Willis Hoover, a missionary in Chile, led an evangelistic campaign in Callao, and in Lima in 1928, which resulted in the formation of the first Pentecostal congregation, led by its own

---

[23] José Luis Pérez Guadalupe, 2004, *Baja a Dios de las nubes. Una alternativa Católica al crecimiento de las "sectas" en América Latina,* Lima: Instituto de Teología Pastoral 'Fray Martín' de la Diócesis de Chosica. 56.

[24] Douglas Jacobsen, 2011, *The World's Christians: Who they are, Where they are, and How they got there,* Chichester: Wiley-Blackwell, 207.

[25] I specialized in the investigation of the Peruvian Israelites of the New Universal Covenant, starting in the year 1978. The new religion grew to number several hundred thousand in Peru and has spread beyond Peru to Latin America, North America, and Europe. I wrote dissertations for three university degrees on the Peruvian Israelites as well as several books in Spanish. The details need not concern us in this short book.

Peruvian pastors. From the beginning of the history of the Assemblies of God in Peru there were divisions and the first schism occurred in 1936, caused by disputes over local autonomy and financial dependence.

In the year 1956 Melvin Hodges, at that time the Missions Secretary of the Assemblies of God in the United States, visited his denomination in Peru. He gave autonomy to the Peruvians and removed most of the missionaries, whose strict control was causing schisms. It is difficult to know exactly but some calculate that there may be as many as seventy Pentecostal denominations in Peru, of which the Assemblies of God continues to be the largest. The Church of God of Peru is another large and active denomination. Its leadership is Peruvian and there are theologians and historians of a high academic standing among its members. On a national level there are some foreign missionaries who seek to exert an influence, while there are other examples, where each Pentecostal church is independent and has little to do with any other, whether evangelical or Pentecostal.

Pentecostalism grew slowly from its beginnings in Peru. So that by 1940 about 25% of Latin American Evangelicals were Pentecostals. As they increased in number and in proportion other evangelicals delayed in accepting them as true Christians with "sound" doctrine. Of course, it was not only a case of recognizing their central doctrines and zeal that concerned Christians, but their charismatic expressions. Nevertheless, while some may have rejected them, others were won over by them to the extent that they ended up joining them.

Samuel Escobar [26] clarifies that before the decade of the 1960s Pentecostals were not accepted in Latin America as equals. Changes came as the World Council of Churches accepted two Chilean Pentecostal denominations into membership in 1961. It was not uncommon for churches like the Lutherans, Baptist, Methodists and Presbyterians to refer to Pentecostals as "sects." In 1966, the famous evangelist Billy Graham called for a World Congress of Evangelization in Berlin that enabled evangelicals to come together in the task of world evangelism. Since then Pentecostal churches

---

[26] Samuel Escobar, 1999, *Tiempo de Misión: América Latina y la misión cristiana hoy,* Santa Fe de Bogotá-Guatemala: Ediciones Clara-Semilla, 70-71.

continued to flourish and some writers are bold enough to claim that they constitute more than 70% of the evangelical population in Peru.

Pentecostalism has taken on distinct forms in many parts of the world. For example, the largest church in Chile, the Pentecostal Methodist Church, practises infant baptism and obeys a Methodist liturgy. Many Pentecostal groups, including some churches in Europe and in Latin America, and most of the charismatics, do not follow a doctrine of "initial evidence" of speaking in tongues. That is, the belief that the initial evidence of a believer receiving the "baptism in the Spirit" is that he/she speaks in other tongues. While classic Pentecostalism defines itself in terms of the doctrine of "initial evidence", numerous Pentecostals do not envisage such a restriction. In the wider context of Pentecostalism, the bigger concern is for an experience of the work of the Holy Spirit and the practice of spiritual gifts.

Walter Hollenweger [27] argues for an Afro-American presence in Pentecostal spirituality. This, he explains, is evident in the oral liturgy, their theology communicated in testimonies, the participation of the entire community in the meetings and worship where visions and dreams came to be common. Meanwhile they added in the element of physical healing through prayer. There is no doubt that they believed in the union of body and mind, linked to the nearness of God in their meetings. The Afro-American liturgy developed with rhythmic hand clapping and in the antiphonal participation of the congregation in the sermons. It is argued that these characteristics are Afro-American in derivation and that they continue almost the same in Pentecostalism everywhere in the world today.

Much more could be written about the origins of Pentecostalism regarding how believers of different races came together as one family of God, based on equality in Christ. With that in view it is wise to remember that the role of women in Pentecostal ministry has always been important. Furthermore, instead of attributing rapid numerical growth to the work of western missionaries, there is no doubt that the thousands of national preachers, both male and female, crossed country after country with a new message "of the power of the Holy Spirit to heal the sick and to cast out demons." While many

---

[27] Walter Hollenweger, 1997, *Pentecostalism: Origins and Developments Worldwide,* Peabody (Massachusetts): Hendrikson Publishers, 18-19.

of these stories have not been written down in books, I remember hearing testimonies, in different local churches, where believers told their stories.

MEMORIES

Over the years I have read how different authors have suggested the "psychological instabilities" present among "neurotic" Pentecostals. Their form of Christianity has been explained as the "refuge of the masses", that is, of the "abandoned poor" who have been "socially marginalised." This so-called "theory of deprivation" is repeated by different authors as the "vision of the dispossessed" who find an "ecstatic religious experience" as a "substitute for success in their social battle." I have always been saddened by such language and approaches. Indeed, even to implore such reasoning does not match up with the makeup of membership across the Pentecostal churches.

Perhaps the fault has also fallen on the attitudes of those of us who have gone from the West of a similar approach, with our exaggerated and almost universal belief, about the superiority of western culture and "civilization." Besides, I wonder whether premillennial eschatology did not play its part by influencing missionaries to "reclaim the nations for Christ", before His imminent return "to set up His kingdom to reign on earth."

The first Pentecostals saw themselves on the verge of a new dispensation. They believed something was wrong with the other churches after having fallen "the original fire from heaven" on the Day of Pentecost. Other churches were by then in a degenerate state. The revival present in Pentecostals at the beginning of the twentieth century, was going to be the "latter rain" promised through the prophet Joel. Consequently, they expected a resurgence of faith in the world, and so "healings and miracles" were but "preludes before the Second Coming of Christ." What is certain is that the phenomenal growth of Pentecostalism has resulted in the fact that there are more Pentecostals in Latin America than in any other continent of the world.

CHAPTER THREE
THEOLOGICAL CHANGE

We are all on spiritual journeys and mine has taken me from Orkney, with initial input from my Baptist roots, to the Birmingham Bible Institute, an interdenominational evangelical college, and from there into a faith mission with much the same ethos. I will always be thankful because at each stage I learned that fellowship is based on our common faith in Jesus Christ. It is a joy to know that I do not need to be particularly concerned about Christian diversity. My own reading of Scripture and contact with the Elim Pentecostal church in Birmingham consolidated my belief in the ongoing presence of spiritual gifts from the Holy Spirit.

When we arrived in 1991 in the Belfast Bible College, with its international and interdenominational staff and student body, that was a good place for me to be. The ethos that primary biblical doctrines are fundamental while secondary issues are there for us to "agree to disagree" appeals to me as healthy. I suppose that I had never really been bothered about secondary issues, not even as a boy. Indeed, my father's practice of seeking fellowship with any person of like faith was part of my psyche. Eighteen years of mission experience in Peru alongside colleagues from diverse backgrounds, and my own reading from historic writers like John Wesley, John Calvin, Martin Luther, and many more-recent Christian writers, have formed me.

For the sake of clarity it is perhaps appropriate at this point to take time and space to affirm that I am an evangelical and that I consider the following cardinal Christian doctrines to be primary: the Trinity, the incarnation of Christ through the virgin birth, the atoning death of Christ, the need for repentance from sin and faith in Jesus Christ to be saved, the resurrection of Jesus Christ from the dead, His ascension to heaven, the presence of the Holy Spirit in every authentic believer and the blessed hope that Christ will return one day to complete the Kingdom of God.

John A Mackay went to Peru in 1916 with the Free Church of Scotland and in 1932 wrote *The Other Spanish Christ*. In that seminal writing he argued that the Christ taken to Peru by the *Conquistadores* in the sixteenth century from Spain had been "born

40

in North Africa" and not in Bethlehem. Where the image of that "dead Christ" dominated the understanding of people, the liberating Gospel of Jesus was needed. In Mackay's 1942 book *A Preface to Christian Theology* he illustrated two different ways of understanding theology. There were those who sat on high balconies at the front of Spanish houses, as it were, watching travellers on the road below. In this way they were theological onlookers without having to regard the practicalities of life. The travellers below, in contrast, faced the problems of life that required, not mere understanding, but called for decision and action. In my journey of faith, I believe I identify more with the travellers.

Mackay writes of personal and "incarnational" mission and that as missionaries, of which I am one, through our service we are given, by the Lord, a platform on which to proclaim our faith. I agree with Mackay that the Church of God is made up of the fellowship of those for whom Jesus Christ is Lord. Indeed, he stated that our collective task "is to make Christians". It has long been my belief that sermons, especially missionary sermons, on the Great Commission often emphasize the word "go", but in Matthew's version of the Great Commission, and in other Gospels, that is not the emphasis at all. Only one verb in Matthew 28:18-20 occurs in the imperative mood, and that is the verb translated "to make disciples". Perhaps it would be better to translate the verse, "Therefore, going, make disciples…" What is important is that Jesus commands His disciples to make disciples. The going is almost taken for granted and refers to wherever we find ourselves in the world as we follow Christ.

A person becomes a disciple when he or she identifies him/herself with the community of those who believe in the Father, Son, and Holy Spirit. This is done through baptism. A person grows as a disciple when he or she is taught everything Jesus commanded. Nowhere does Jesus mention a person being evangelized, becoming a Christian, being converted, or joining a church or denomination. Jesus does not command His disciples to do any of those things. Rather, He tells them to make disciples, a longer, but more complete process. It continues down to our time and until "the very end of the age": disciples are to make disciples. That would sound like a daunting proposition without Jesus' encouraging words, "I am with you always." The One who possesses all authority in heaven and on earth promises to always be with His disciples as they carry out His mission to make disciples. What might sound unachievable is now seen to be certain.

THE LAW IN SCRIPTURE

The one area in Scripture that I had to come to terms with on my journey was the Law of God. The Ten Commandments were given to Moses and are summarized in Scriptures such as Exodus 20:3-17 and Deuteronomy 5:6-21. This is rightly presented as God's required behaviour for humanity. Jesus further summarized God's Law as requiring perfect love for God and for one's neighbour (Matthew 22:35-40). Some teach and believe that a right relationship with God can be attained through performance of the Law, or that this was so in another dispensation. Yet Paul challenges this in Galatians 2:16[28]. There are Christians who believe that God gave the Law to provide a way to live victoriously and to receive blessing.

A closer examination of Scripture confirmed to me that God did not give the Law so that people could become right with Him based upon their lawful behaviour. Neither is lawful behaviour the way to remain right with God. A right relationship with God is a settled gift because of what God did through Christ. This should lead to living right, but salvation cannot be earned by right behaviour. It is a gift of God.

This begs the question as to why God gave the Law. The first answer is that God gave the Law to reveal our sin. Romans 3:20[29] reveals God's Law as a mirror reflecting the fact that we all fall short of what God expects. Secondly, the Law convinces us that we are "locked up" (Romans 11:32), as in prison, unable to hit the mark expected of us. God's Law does not give us peace with God. Instead, God's Law imprisons us and leaves us in a state of missing the mark. Thirdly, Paul writes that the purpose of the Law is to lead us to Christ who, through His work of grace on the cross, might "have mercy upon all" (Romans 11:32). Once this is accomplished the

---

[28] "Knowing that a man is not justified by works of the Law but by faith in Jesus Christ, even we have believed in Jesus Christ, that we might be justified by faith in Christ and not by works of the Law; for by the works of the Law no flesh shall be justified."

[29] "Therefore, by the deeds of the Law no flesh will be justified in His sight, for by the Law is the knowledge of sin."

purpose of the Law has been fulfilled. This is made clear by Paul in Galatians 3:23-25:

> *But before faith came, we were kept under guard [imprisoned] by the Law, kept for the faith which afterward would be revealed. Therefore, the Law was our tutor to bring us to Christ, that we might be justified by faith. But after faith has come, we are no longer under a tutor.*

The Greek word for "tutor" is *paidagogos*, which means "child disciplinarian." This person was hired by parents to escort their children to school. Whenever a child veered from the path, the "tutor" would hit the child with a long stick. The children were literally driven to school like cattle. Once at school, however, where the real schoolmaster was, the job of the *paidagogos* was over. The tutor's job was to lead a child to the true place of learning. Just as the *paidagogos* would keep children on the right path and "drive" them to school, the Law acts as our "tutor" to drive us to Christ. As we wander off the path, the Law explicitly reminds us that we do not measure up to God's standard. The Law prods us back onto the path that leads us to a right relationship with Christ.

Perhaps I can summarize our relationship to God in the words of the Apostle Paul in Colossians 2:6: "As you therefore have received Christ Jesus the Lord, so walk in Him." We are to walk the same way we came in! As we did not come into our relationship with Jesus based on good behaviour, we did not earn God's approval by trying hard. We trusted in Jesus and freely received God's grace. So it is that we continue looking to Jesus as the basis for our vindication and validation. The Christian life really is, first and foremost, a struggle to simply, purely, "trust in Christ." We continue to rest, as we did in the beginning of our Christian walk, in what God had done and promises to do. This is the focus of our true spiritual journey.

GIVING

I suspect I am like many other Christians. I ask myself if I am practising grace, allowing the Spirit of grace to live through me in such a way that I help lift oppressive weights off others and spiritually empower them to live? Or am I trying to force people to live under laws, rules or formulas for a spirituality that causes them to feel weighed down and unable to live up to those standards? Is not our spiritual journey characterised by our attempts to avoid licence on the one hand and legalism on the other? We believe that faith in Jesus plus anything else is not faith. This oppressive weight we place ourselves under is called legalism. Legalists push religious performance as the means to a right standing with God. All Christians need to be on our guard against the subtle use of "formulas" and doctrines that are so often used to press good people of the faith into conformity with a religious system instead of conformity to Christ.

I have witnessed the use of Scripture to cajole believers into giving[30], both as an obligation and with the promise of receiving from the Lord. Giving is not designed to get us on God's good side, nor do we give to stay on His good side, nor do we give to get more back from God. Sadly, it may be true that wrong teaching on this subject could motivate people to give by appealing to their greed. It may even emphasise that we "owe it" to our church. It is a fact that tithing is so important in many churches in Peru, that if a member fails to tithe, he/she faces church discipline, or excommunication. That never sat easily with me.

The concept of tithing hardly appears in the New Testament, and then only in a negative light (Matthew 23:23; Luke 18:9-12). Tithing originated in the Old Testament. There were three separate tithes that totalled about 27%: 10% for the Levites; 10% of what remained to support the national festivals; and 10% of the rest for the poor. This was non-optional giving. Back then the Israelites had a form of government called a theocracy, which means they were under the rule of God and the religious system. These tithes simply amounted to "tax monies" needed to run the country. The 27 percent it cost to live in that church-state may be compared to the amount of taxes we pay to live in our democracy.

Giving is, and has always been, an issue of the heart. Exodus 25 relates the account of raising the financial resources to construct the

---

[30] For example: Malachi 3:8: "Will a man rob God? Yet you have robbed Me! But you say, 'In what way have we robbed You?' In tithes and offerings." Luke 6:38: "Give, and it will be given you: good measure, pressed down, shaken together, and running over will be put into your bosom. For with the same measure that you use, it will be measured back to you." 2 Corinthians 9:6: "But this I say: He who sows sparingly will also reap sparingly, and he who sows bountifully will also reap bountifully."

sanctuary. God said to Moses: "Speak to the children of Israel, that they may bring Me an offering. From everyone who gives it willingly with his heart you shall take my offering" (v.2). After almost ten chapters of specifications concerning the sanctuary, Moses repeats the conditions of the giving. In Exodus 35 Moses speaks to the people: "This is the thing which the Lord commanded, saying: 'Take from among you an offering to the Lord. Whoever is of a willing heart…'" (vs.4-5).

In 2 Corinthians 9:7 Paul writes: "You must each decide in your heart how much to give. And do not give reluctantly or in response to pressure. For God loves a person who gives cheerfully." In the following verse, Paul reveals the source from which a heart to give comes: "And God will generously provide all you need. Then you will always have everything you need, and plenty left over to share with others." To believe that verse should result in giving from the heart.

I have no wish to make a list of things that we should and should not do. That would defeat the purpose as each Christian must decide regarding secondary issues. The only concept I wish to tackle here is that of tithing because of what I was led to reconsider in a cultural context of poverty in Peru. I had always tithed, that is, I always gave one tenth of what I earned to the church and to church ministries. I still do so. In the light of what the primitive church was taught in Scripture, as outlined above, I came to another conclusion, especially regarding the poor. The legalist will always want to see another punished or made to perform as a compensation for perceived weakness or sin.

Finally, for those who give to get, in Romans 11:35 Paul asks a rhetorical question: "Or who has first given to Him and it shall be repaid to him?" The answer is that no one has really given to God because all things come from Him. It is true that we do reap what we sow in a spiritual sense and there are rewards for good works. But if we sow or work to earn a reward, or to put God in a position of owing us, we get nothing. God owes us nothing. And Matthew 6:1-4 relates that if we give to be noticed or to gain someone's approval, we have our reward already. In other words, we have been "receipted" in full, and our only reward is that someone noticed.

THE LORD'S SUPPER

The first time I ever shared in the Lord's Supper was one day after my sixteenth birthday on the 31st January 1965 in the Kirkwall Baptist Church in Orkney. It meant a great deal to me then and now I have come to appreciate the experience even more. The one thing offered by Christianity that no other religion offers, is forgiveness. True forgiveness is based on the atoning death of Christ. Not only so, but our own ability to forgive others emanates from the cross of Christ and is our response to the Lord. We read in Matthew 18:21-22: "Then Peter came to Him and said, 'Lord, how often shall my brother sin against me, and I forgive him? Up to seven times?' Jesus said to him, 'I do not say to you, up to seven times, but up to seventy times seven.'"

The symbolism of the celebration of the Lord's Supper today is significant for me on several levels. The foremost is that of the death of Christ. Quite clearly the sacrament of communion is a symbol of the death of Christ and when we, the body of Christ on earth meet, we give thanks for the tremendous sacrifice that Jesus made so we might enter into God's family. Secondly, we thank God for the blood of the covenant that assures us that absolutely nothing can separate us from the love of God in Christ Jesus. Thirdly, we share in a symbol that represents the forgiveness of all our sins. Fourthly, and I love this part, the symbol of our response to Christ, by taking [the bread and wine], by eating and drinking, and by sharing with all gathered for the occasion. We take, eat, drink and in our hearts respond to Christ by faith, with thanksgiving. Finally, the symbols represent the joys of heaven.

I look forward with anticipation to celebrating the Lord's Supper with my fellow believers because everything we need in Jesus Christ is there represented. His body was broken for us, His blood was shed for us, once and for all time. There is a new and living way into God's presence so that we, the body of Christ, belong to God forever. Our sins have been washed away, every single one of them. As we take, as we eat and, as we drink, we trust in Christ and "proclaim His atoning death." We go on feeding on Christ in our hearts by faith "until He comes." Something happens each time we do so, until we share with Him perfectly, and forever in Heaven itself.

CHAPTER FOUR
NEW RELIGIOUS MOVEMENTS

I enjoyed academic study in the University of Aberdeen [31] from which I graduated with the degrees of Master of Letters (1981) and Doctor of Philosophy (1989). After return to Peru with Baptist Missions, in early 2000, I enrolled, at-a-distance, with the University of Wales, Lampeter, through the Irish Baptist College, for a Master of Arts in Theology in 2003, graduating in December 2005. After Jeannie and I left Peru "for good" at the end of 2007, I worked only three days each week in the Irish Baptist College as Director of Post Graduate studies [32], I enrolled again in the University of Wales, Lampeter for a Licence in Theology. My idea was to update myself in theological studies and pursue more recent research, culminating, as in all the above qualifications, with a dissertation on New Religious Movements.

My area of specialization allowed me to teach a module at postgraduate level in the Lima Evangelical Seminary on Peruvian New Religious Movements. After we moved as a family to Belfast in 1991, I taught modules on New Religious Movements at both undergraduate and postgraduate levels in the Queen's University of Belfast. On return to Peru in the year 2000 with Baptist Missions I enabled the Baptist Seminary in Tacna to be established and again ventured into teaching my specialization there. I felt that I had pushed the boat out too far for that audience regarding my approach

---

[31] I was physically present, along with my family, in Aberdeen from September 1978 until May 1979 and again from September 1980 until September 1981. This culminated in the completion of the Master of Letters in Primal Religion, awarded in December 1981. I registered there for a PhD in January 1985, while on furlough, returning to Peru in early March of 1985. During the following years I was constantly doing research into the Peruvian new religion, the Israelites of the New Universal Covenant. By the end of 1987, my archive was as full as it was going to be. As the department in which I enrolled for the PhD had moved to the University of Edinburgh I completed the thesis in that city but graduated in July 1989 through the University of Aberdeen, after returning to Peru at the end of 1988.

[32] From January 2008 until January 2010, after which I worked part-time for IBC and part-time for Baptist Missions until retirement in January 2014.

to the study of other religious groups, so dedicated myself largely to other projects[33].

I will always be grateful that I was able to stretch myself academically and learn a methodology of research that changed my approach to scholarly study. Religious Studies, as an academic discipline, included socio-anthropological investigative methodology. These tools were used in the study of New Religious Movements. As an evangelical Christian I encountered a freedom to approach other religions without an initial interest in proving their "heresies." I imbibed a more objective methodology that allowed me to "place in parenthesis" my own faith while I was pursuing field research. At that stage I resisted temptations to emit theological judgements until I had completed more thorough investigation. That enabled me to discover what "was believed" in another religion, rather than "what I thought they believed." Finally, this freed me up to make my "value judgements" in the light of the uniqueness of Christ and the Gospel.

This approach presented the possibility of practising "participant observation", while at the same time suspending judgement on groups that might be envisaged as suspect to many Christians. Given that we Christians are prone to placing labels on fellow Christians I found this approach helpful. These are the premises behind this chapter. I have placed "in parenthesis" some of my own "value judgements" long enough. I state this, I trust with grace, because I have learned from groups that are different from where I am at in my "journey" of faith. I invite you to join me as I reflect and make some of what I dare to call "creative evaluations."

Before I record some of my "observations" on those in other groups, I start by observing myself. I could not go on in life without my faith in the cross of Christ. By that I mean that I discover, on my journey through life, sinfulness in me that I did not know anything about. Without the work of Christ on the cross to cover all that, I would despair because I am sure that in the depths of my heart there remains unknown corruption. With passing years, I am forced to acknowledge the deceptive power of sin. I turn back to Christ when I see that I am tempted to justify my own desires, when they are not in

---

[33] Firstly, to establish a Baptist Seminary in Tacna, then to set up *Radio El Sembrador,* and, finally, to oversee extensive building programmes.

tune with His. There is something elusive in my walk with God that battles against what I read in Scripture. I thank God for every moment of victory by the grace of God through the cross. The Lord enables me, by His Spirit, to subjugate my flesh. Scripture reminds me that "Christ died for the ungodly" and that I am "justified by His blood" (Romans 5:6, 9). I face each day anew, a sinner justified and free!

SOME OBSERVATIONS

Over the years I have witnessed authority movements periodically sweeping through the church. What has always concerned me are the common threads and variations of the same trends. Visions and guidance figure large and come from spiritual heads, pastors, elders, group leaders, husbands etc. What makes me sad is that it is possible for those who depend on the above so easily to fail to trust in the Lord and hear from Him, in His Word. The glory of the priesthood of every believer in Christ is in danger of being lost in the mix. It is too easy for us all to lose sight of the grace of God in Christ.

As Christians we are those who acknowledge the authority of Christ and as we read Scripture understand the amazement of those who first heard Jesus. Like them we know and marvel because no one else teaches like Him, with such authority. The Scriptures separate Him out from the Scribes and Pharisees of His day. His authority is in the truth of what He taught. Is that not what we also believe? The authority is in the truth of Scripture, God's inspired Word. This undergirds everything else.

A first concern in any group must be the distinction between truth and error regarding the teaching of Scripture. It is important for me to integrate my faith and my discipline. In practise I must wear a hat of an objective student of religion, and the hat of a concerned evangelical Christian. There is a place in life to bring a clearly Christian or biblical critique to bear on any religious group, Christian, or otherwise. Thus I came to feel it very important to find out what any particular group really believes, what it is really doing, what the logic of its inner working is, why it seems so strange to us that people do the things they do. Before I critique any specific group, I need to find out what it really believes and, what its side of the story on a point of controversy is. Such checking is of great importance to me.

Some Christians assume that Pentecostalism is a heresy and treat anyone who "smacks of it" as heretics. In my Christian worldview, while I have always declared that I am not Pentecostal, [I apologize for the use of "labels" here] it is not for me to point a finger at them and treat them as heretical. I neither believe that nor have I experienced that when it comes to sharing fellowship. Pentecostals are my brothers and sisters in Christ. In passing, I believe the gifts of the Spirit continue in the Church today. I can live with the fallout that may result from that clarification. At the same time, I also recognize my own differences.

Although groups vary a great deal one from another, they also have some patterns of behaviour and certain characteristics that apply to most, if not all, of them. I am interested in recurring patterns of behaviour regarding leadership, the recruitment and socialization of members, as well as with many other areas of religious life. I see the differences, but I also see the similarities. The kind of patterns that concern me would be, first of all, a strong authoritarian presence, an emphasis on the leader/founder, a focal emphasis on the leader's teachings, and the election of the leaders to a very high position of respect, sometimes bordering on deity. From the Christian perspective, this is obviously a departure from revealed truth as we understand it, and in that sense a pattern of false teaching.

Another common trait would be the element of control over the lives of members. Even in groups that call themselves Christian one can see these same characteristics of control and manipulation. I see a theme of elitism, an exclusivist orientation, not only in their teachings, but also in their conveying of a sense of superiority, that is linked perhaps to their view of their own group as being central to history. They tend to hold people in dependence and adolescence rather than assisting them to grow toward maturity and adulthood.

Despite what I wrote earlier, it is not always wise to be "value free" in our approach. It may be a trap to fall for the public relations pitch of seeking to downplay certain behaviour when confronted with evidence of deceit. We need to let people know where we are coming from as Christians. On the other hand, I do not believe that approaching a member of a group with insults about them, or their leaders, insults that question the integrity of anyone who would join them, is either helpful, or particularly Christian. We have two tasks. We have the task of reporting accurately the negative facts that are facts. We also need to track down false rumours that have been presented as facts.

It may be a truism to suggest we have an increasing religiously naïve public. Vacuums exist, and into that vacuum come new religious movements. This is not a surprising development. The attitude of adoration is evident even in the groups that do not view their leaders as divine. Nominal Christians are most vulnerable and much has been written about the so-called shepherding movement. Christians who feel a deficiency in mainstream evangelical churches commit elsewhere. People are looking for a measure of reality, truth, and spiritual experience. We may not agree with what they ultimately will achieve in terms of membership in these groups and the "truth" that they receive. They are looking for the perfect church, the perfect pastor. They become spiritual butterflies. The doctrinal or belief system of any given group is almost always secondary in the decision to sign on.

The primary reasons that people are attracted to religious groups may be social in nature. They are attracted to the sense of family, of community, and of purpose that these groups capitalize on. Doctrinal considerations are overshadowed by personal considerations. Indoctrination into the teachings of the group comes later. This all has implications for the way many evangelical Christians approach the topic of what we have termed "cults." We have traditionally emphasized doctrinal differences and distinctives. This may still be crucial, but we must learn to look at the whole spectrum of variables that are part of the decision to join a "cult." These include psychological, sociological, and personal needs. The search is for a "place to belong." Is this search so wrong?

There is a topic that, in my view needs mention. It concerns the distinction between the gifts of God's Holy Spirit and what I would call the counterfeit gifts or the counterfeit miracles that are performed by people who are empowered by Satan and his emissaries. When we look at the New Testament evidences of supernaturalism, that power comes from one of two sources: God the Holy Spirit or Satan, and not from some human power. Every Christian leader is entrusted with the Gospel of Christ to distinguish God's truth from the work of God's adversary, Satan. Not everyone who claims to proclaim truth is preaching God's Truth.

In some so-called Christian groups, there is an incredible preoccupation with the demonic. It is popular these days for people to cast out demons – from unbelievers as well as from Christians. I do believe in the reality of demons and the necessity of spiritual warfare. I also believe in the need for exorcism and that the Lord equips some people to counsel and work in this difficult area. What I observe is that there is a disturbing tendency in these marginal groups to emphasize the power and activity of Satan more than the victorious work of Christ. That is a matter for pause and concern.

I take Paul very seriously when he says that which is not of faith is sin. I see non-Christian religions as being outside the faith. I think it is a sad commentary on the time in which we live when we have reached the point where we do not, in most contexts, have the freedom to evaluate other groups in terms of our own particular perspective and faith, lest we get threatened with a lawsuit, or become targets of harassment. When we use labels these days, it is necessary to be careful and sensitive. More mutual respect is needed. Whatever label we use to define a group, there needs to be increased information before we can make statements, evaluative or otherwise, about them.

We need objective, accurate information. We need to help people see that God's truth is as it is revealed in His Word, and the relationship of that truth to our everyday lives, and the necessity and possibility of having a personal relationship with Jesus Christ. It has been my experience that, rather than spending a great deal of time arguing with people or even engaging in discussions of a strictly biblical nature, we need to impress upon people the reality of a personal encounter with the God of the Bible. That really gets through. An aggressive, confrontational approach is not, in my opinion, the way to go. I think we need to be patient, and we need to be prepared for a continuing dialogue. It is not something that will happen overnight. Our attitude is so important. We must accept people as persons and affirm their basic search. Then they will be more open to what we have to say.

CONCLUSIONS

It is easy to become so tolerant that we fail to discern and distinguish that which, from a biblical position, clearly demonstrates error. What truth is denied, or substituted, or ignored, or out of balance? We need to share our Christian convictions in love and identify those distinctions that we hold dear. But loving people does not save them. People must come to see their sin and then appropriate the grace of Christ Jesus.

The Scriptures as contained in the Bible undergird any questions that I ask. The preaching of the cross of Christ is central to any evaluation of a so-called Christian group. A call to follow Christ should include repentance, a call to live a holy life, but also to anticipate suffering in life, albeit with the promise of God to walk with us through the difficult times. This latter element is important because the New Testament differentiates present blessings, and trials, from the ultimate perfection of heaven. Indeed, on that level our task is to warn about the judgement to come, but to avoid declaring damnation on anyone. That task is placed in greater hands than ours'.

I have been blessed lately by two different pastors (one Presbyterian and the other Anglican), when preaching about the New Testament Scribes and Pharisees, admitted to being like them at times. That was liberating. Jesus loves His church! He will send people who see the need to speak the truth, to lift the load, to heal the sheep. By His Spirit and through His Word, He will call and convict and draw to Himself. The result will be brokenness, mourning, and repentance and that always brings life and restoration. I continue to call out to the Lord and welcome back the grace of God again. God loves to give grace to people like me when I know that I need it.

As we seek to commit to a local church there are principles in Scripture that are placed there to guide us. The authority of a church is in God's truth. We submit to that authority when it demonstrates authenticity. That truth finally resides in God through Jesus Christ. Every Christian already has received God's approval through Christ and His death on the cross. Following on from this, questions of church government, obligations for members, the intended impact on the world, the view of God, the authority of those "in charge", and whether, as we read our Bibles, we discern that we are called in a similar manner, and to the same purposes that the others sense for themselves, then we may join that church.

CHAPTER FIVE
THE MISSIONARY

PREAMBLE

With the privilege of hindsight as a septuagenarian two aspects of my life now come to the fore. Firstly, I am surprised by the variety of tasks I ended up doing as a full-time missionary. They were all enriching but had not been anticipated as steps along the way. Secondly, issues of "call" and guidance were more varied and mundane than in the missionary biographies I read as a boy. Paul's reflection in 1 Corinthians 13:11-12 reminds me to recognize both the wisdom that comes with years and the need for humility as we seek to follow an all-wise God. Paul wrote:

> *When I was a child, I spoke and thought and reasoned as a child. But when I grew up, I put away childish things. Now we see things imperfectly, like puzzling reflections in a mirror, but then we will see everything with perfect clarity. All that I know now is partial and incomplete, but then I will know everything completely, just as God now knows me completely.*

I still identify myself as a missionary. For that reason, this chapter is important to me and represents a lifetime of reflections. Too many books, authors, colleagues, students, and cultural experiences have shaped my thinking for me to be able to acknowledge them all. Jeannie and I could never have anticipated the rich variety of experiences that were to ensue. What follows is not designed to be an academic and theological lecture[34] on the subject. My intention is to articulate my own conclusions as I see them now. I trust they are, though "partial and incomplete", practical for other fellow-Christians who venture into mission and into life.

My early desire to be a missionary was never lost from sight as I prepared to travel to Peru. After reaching Peru in 1974, an initial period of church planting in the Andean towns of Abancay and Chalhuanca, was, from 1977, soon mixed with teaching in a rural

---

[34] Some of the material has been taken from parts of my "Biblical and Theological Basis of Mission" course (2008-2013), taught as an elective to second year undergraduate degree students, in the Irish Baptist College in Moira, Northern Ireland.

Bible Institute. I continued academic studies on each consecutive furlough in the University of Aberdeen. In lieu of financial support and bread on the table, I was variously occupied, on consecutive furloughs, both in Scotland and in the USA, as a pastor, a part-time farmer and chicken house builder. In 1981 Jeannie and I, along with our two children, were introduced to a once-a-year post-graduate teaching slot in the Missiology Department of the Lima Evangelical Seminary [35]. This pattern continued for several years and was interspersed with field leadership. By 1985 we moved to Lima and ministry included preaching, teaching in different theological institutions as well as field leadership. In late 1991 Belfast became our home and as our children grew, Jeannie and I both enjoyed busy roles in the Belfast Bible College[36].

This was followed by eight years of service in Baptist Missions in Tacna, Peru (2000-2007). It was a joy to be able to set up the Baptist Seminary and a Radio Station in the city. Jeannie came into her own as she established a Women's Study Fellowship (as in the Belfast Bible College) in the Seminary, a small bookshop and ordered the Seminary library. My time there also involved me in being a project manager as I oversaw several large building projects. My official working life came to an end in January 2014 with a role as part-time Post-Graduate Director in the Irish Baptist College (2008-2014) and then (2010-2014), in addition, as part-time Mission Promoter for Baptist Missions. Jeannie returned to her love of books and was employed in the Faith Mission bookshop in Lisburn. Since leaving Peru "for good" in late 2007 I returned twenty times. After retirement in early 2014 I continued to visit Peru and, for three years, both started and handed over, a charity for the support of destitute children in Tacna.

---

[35] I thank Dr G. Stewart McIntosh for offering this opportunity. I taught one post-graduate module in missiology and supervised several dissertations. My area of speciality was the study of New Religious Movements in Primal Societies. One of my dissertation students, the late Rubén Zavala, published his research as *La Historia de Las Asambleas de Dios del Perú,* 1989.

[36] I was employed as a full-time lecturer and Director of Studies. After studying for three years in the Women's Study Fellowship, Jeannie was then asked to head up the programme.

THE MISSIONARY

I am embarrassed to confess that, over the years, I have both recorded attempts at defining the word "missionary" and, to my shame, used some of them as I taught. One such is: "Missionaries are very human folks, just doing what they are asked. Simply a bunch of nobodies trying to exalt Somebody." This, I now recognize, is almost meaningless and, equally so is the idea, mentioned in the introduction to this book, that every Christian is either a missionary or a mission field. It is true that every Christian should be involved in witnessing about Christ by word and deed[37], but to state that every believer is a missionary would mean that there is no special role of missionary in the church.

At the same time, I reject the exclusive idea that anyone who receives financial support from individuals and/or churches, to be involved in Christian activity, is a missionary. There are obviously many people who earn their own livelihood and yet qualify as missionaries. Finally, if we reduce missions to cross-cultural church planting, we also exclude many who are involved in work that should be considered "missionary". But then, just what is a missionary? This is a difficult question to answer.

For convenience I include the following definition of missionary:

> *In the technical and traditional sense of the word, a missionary is a Christian messenger of the gospel of Jesus Christ, sent forth by the authority of the Lord and the church to cross national borders and/or cultural and religious lines in order to occupy new frontiers for Christ, to preach the gospel of redemption in Christ Jesus unto the salvation of people, to make disciples and to establish functioning and evangelizing Christian churches according to the command of Christ and the example of the apostles.*

A question stemming from the fact the apostles and other itinerant preachers were engaged in evangelism, is whether the role of evangelist is the missionary gift. The Latin speaking church of the second century referred to their evangelists as missionaries. However, we should notice that the New Testament demonstrates considerable overlap between the gifts. All apostles possessed the

---

[37] Tekmito Adegemo wrote: "We cannot preach good news and be bad news."

gifts of evangelism and teaching. Yet, not all evangelists were apostles. Philip was not one. What is true regarding apostles and evangelists is also true of apostles, evangelists, and pastor-teachers (or pastors and teachers)[38]. Many pastor-teachers remained in one area to teach the church there. Timothy, with a reasonably settled teaching ministry, is encouraged to do the work of an evangelist.

Perhaps it would be better if we did not restrict the missionary gift to any one of the spiritual gifts mentioned in the Bible. This is supported by the fact that there is some overlap between the gifts, and that none of the lists of gifts in the Scripture seems to be complete. Mission is accomplished through evangelism (performed by apostles, evangelists, and others), by uniting people to the people of God through faith in Christ, and by teaching people the whole counsel of God as revealed in the Bible. Seen in this way the four (or five) foundational gifts mentioned in Ephesians 4:11 would all be counted as missionary gifts, as all serve to build up the church in quantity as well as quality.

Into this mix I wish to mention the missionary "call." On the one side are those who would state: "If you are not called to stay, you are called to go!" Is this not another meaningless cliché? Similarly, others claim: "Do not be a missionary if you can possibly avoid it." Perhaps the idea of a call to missionary work should be indistinguishable from a call to any other vocation. A person prepares accordingly. For others, the fact that the Bible commands us to "make disciples…" impels them to seek cross-cultural ministry. The idea prevails that God would give a Pauline "Damascus Road experience" or a "Macedonian vision" if He wants somebody to become a missionary. With these different ideas about the missionary call in circulation it is helpful to go back and see what the Bible has to say about the concept of receiving a call.

The place to start is with the stark fact that, although the Bible refers to several different types of calls, it nowhere mentions a call to missions. Most of the calls in the Bible relate to live the Christian life and not calls to perform any kind of Christian service. There is a call

---

[38] See Ephesians 4:11: "Now these are the gifts Christ gave to the church: the apostles, the prophets, the evangelists, and the pastors and teachers."

to salvation. There is a call to repentance[39]. There is a call to discipleship. There is a call to holiness. There is a call to freedom[40]. There is a call to live in peace[41]. But there is no call to be a missionary. Part of this has to do with the fact that the Bible does not refer to missionaries as we usually think of them. The New Testament mentions apostles, prophets, evangelists, and pastor/teachers, but not missionaries.

The "calls" given to certain individuals in Scripture so that they could do some specific ministry are few and far between. To think of them as normative or necessary is to go far beyond what we find in the Bible. It would be better for us to think of a "call" as being a much more ordinary way for God to reveal His will that could be received by anyone who is open to God's work in their lives. Bruce Waltke's definition of "call" is very helpful in this regard: "A call is an inner desire given by the Holy Spirit, through the Word of God and confirmed by the community of Christ."

Although we often refer to our call to a specific country or missionary organization, the Bible is silent about such a possibility. The closest that we can come to any such concept in the New Testament is Paul's statement that God called Peter to be an apostle to the Jews and Paul to be an apostle to the Gentiles (Gal. 2:6-9). Their individual tasks lay in those general directions. However, from their actions, we know that this never restricted them from preaching to anyone. Peter served in Samaria and took the gospel to Cornelius. Paul made it his practice to go to the Jews first. Even their specific callings were more to preach than to do so in any one place or to any one specific group of people.

This should alert us to the fact that the distinction between home missions and foreign missions is unknown in Scripture. In Acts 1:8 Jesus told His disciples they would be His witnesses "in Jerusalem, and in all Judea and Samaria, and to the ends of the earth." All places

---

[39] See Luke 5:32: "I have come to call not those who think they are righteous, but those who know they are sinners and need to repent."

[40] See Galatians 5:13: "For you have been called to freedom, my brothers and sisters. But do not use your freedom to satisfy your sinful nature. Instead, use your freedom to serve one another in love."

[41] See 1 Corinthians 7:15b: "… for God has called you to live in peace."

are equally important, and all should be evangelized at the same time. As is often repeated, "The need does not constitute the call." The call comes from God to preach the Word. The determination of place comes either through the direct leading of the Holy Spirit in some way, general circumstances, or by personal choice. The determination of destination, missionary society, people group, ministry etc., is therefore probably better considered under the heading of guidance rather than of call.

By modifying the idea of a missionary call, those who state that they have not received one, or are not sure, or do not want to receive one, cannot simply excuse themselves from missions because God did not make it patently clear to them that He wanted them to go. Things may change. Similarly, no one who is involved in Christian ministry should develop the attitude that since they are preaching in a church, teaching in a Bible College, doing street evangelism or whatever, do not have to consider the possibility of going somewhere where there is a greater need for their gifting to be used. Also, we can better communicate the need for Christians, who have not received a "call" into full-time ministry, to work both at home and abroad to enhance the spread of the gospel.

Most mission agencies are crying out for people who have many different kinds of spiritual gifts as well as academic and practical training that can be used to set free evangelists, church planters, and Bible teachers so that they can make disciples. Administrators, teachers of missionary children, medical personnel, language teachers, trades people, and other professionals, are greatly needed.

The same Spirit who led Paul to serve in various locations can also lead people today to serve in different places. Pastors change churches. Missionaries change fields, and at times even return to their "home" to serve God there. A salutary conclusion is that this makes it possible for more people to consider whether they should go into missions themselves. The important principle is that instead of waiting for a "call", a person should look for guidance from the Lord.

RECOGNIZING GOD'S GUIDANCE

It is one thing to say that God guides certain people into full-time preaching or teaching ministry of the Word, it is another thing to ascertain how He does this. Let it be said that just as God used different means to guide people in Bible times, He still uses different means today. The ways God informed Moses, Isaiah, and Timothy that He wanted them to serve Him were very distinct. To insist that He must use only one of these methods today makes little sense. How then does God guide us?

Few, if any of us, will ever have a crisis experience, like Moses in the desert, Isaiah when he saw the vision of God, or Paul on the road to Damascus. God could use a combination of factors, a phone call, a sermon, a conversation, a tragedy, or a growing inner conviction to lead a person. Through reading the Bible we learn of God and of His heart for the world. As we become more like His Son Jesus, we may find that our heart aches for the world and that we want to do something so that others might be saved.

Missionary biographies are of value. It is surprising how many missionaries of my generation have been influenced by the lives of people such as David Brainerd, Hudson Taylor, Amy Carmichael, Gladys Aylward, and Jim Elliot. I was influenced when I read Elizabeth Elliot's account of her first husband's death at the hands of the Aucas in Ecuador. Her quotation from Jim Elliot's diary made a lasting impact on my life. He wrote: "He is no fool who gives that which he cannot keep, to gain what he cannot lose." Another powerful life-changing statement was made by Abraham Kuyper: "There is not an inch of any sphere of life over which Jesus Christ does not say, 'Mine'".

If missionary biographies are important, so is the influence of godly people we know. Parents, pastors, Sunday School teachers, and missionaries are all used of God to stir up a love for the world in the hearts of many people. I testify to both the influence of missionary biographies and to the influence of godly people on my direction in life and spiritual growth.

God arranges circumstances. This might be in the form of a crisis, a one-off opportunity to speak to someone, the thrill of leading one person to Christ which gives the desire to tell others about Him, or something else. Several of the points already mentioned have given a hint of the need to be concerned for the eternal welfare of other people. It should be stated that if someone is not burdened for the souls of others that they should not even consider becoming a missionary. Paul could write that "I am compelled to preach. Woe to me if I do not preach the gospel!" (1 Corinthians 9:16). Many missionaries confess to feeling the same.

Personal recognition of at least some of the gifts needed to perform the task is essential. One does not have to be a brilliant biblical expositor to be a missionary. What one does need is some gift, some talent, some skill, some training, that will be of use for the spreading of the gospel. It is important to remember that the skill in question may be one that is needed to free evangelists and church planters to do their jobs.

In addition to having a "feeling" that God wants a person to be a missionary is the need for the leaders of one's home church to recognize that they have the gifts necessary to serve in this way. When Paul and Barnabas were sent out by the church of Antioch, the Holy Spirit revealed to the men involved and to the church that He had set them apart for that task. If God wants a person to be a missionary, He will not hide it from the Christian community that knows them best.

Most of those who enter full-time missionary service will acknowledge that God used a good number of different factors to guide them into missions. In many cases it is the cumulative effect of these events working together that confirm God's guidance. However, it is unlikely that God is going to give a person complete assurance that he or she is so guided. To do so would extinguish the need for faith. There comes a time for those who believe they are led by God to step out, to trust fully that it is God's will.

Sometimes God does lead people through dramatic events, such as when Paul had the vision of the man from Macedonia begging him to come over into Macedonia to help those who lived there. Paul and those serving with him immediately prepared to leave for Macedonia, concluding that God had opened a door for them to preach the gospel there (Acts 16:9-10).

At other times, God leads through much less dramatic means, such as in Acts chapter 15, the chapter before the dramatic Macedonian "call." After the people at headquarters in Jerusalem had settled the theological dispute, they wanted to let the churches know their decision. Then it "seemed good" to the apostles, to the elders and to the whole church to send Paul, Barnabas, Judas, and Silas to take their letter to Antioch (Acts 15:22). Thus, these four men received their guidance as to what to do and where to go through what "seemed good" to the leaders in Jerusalem.

In their letter, the leaders wrote that they were agreed that it "seemed good" for them to send the men with the letter to explain it. They went on to write that it "seemed good" to the Holy Spirit as well as to them to not overburden them with too many rules (Acts 15:25-28). In these cases, people received their guidance to service through what "seemed good" to others. (Note: Although several recent paraphrases use different words in verses 22, 25, and 28, the same Greek word is used in all three, and the most common translation of it is, "seemed good.")

CONCLUSIONS

As a missionary I believe that, in the Lord's good pleasure, He gave me the vision for a diversity of projects over decades. I had learned after years in ministry in Peru to no longer be involved in too many ministries. It had cost my family a heavy price. It seemed wiser to dedicate my effort to one "new" effort at one given time. Prayer preceded the designing, raising funds, and the implementation of each succeeding ministry. It was a joy to fulfil each vision through human and material resources. My idea was always to move on and to hand things on. There is always a right time to do so. I confess that it was especially difficult when I sensed that folk, who did not always share the same vision, nor had expended much effort, new to the task, jostled for a position. More than once I pulled back before the ministry had been sufficiently established.

In part it was a battle with pride. In fact, I need to testify – confession is good for the soul - that three times over as many decades I lost my cool with someone. I knew that there could never be an excuse for such behaviour, irrespective of the other person. I decided, on each occasion, that it was time and right to pull back. I also sought to both ask for and freely offer forgiveness, both from the Lord and from the person. A bad taste is left in the mouth after such an experience. There are two ways to get rid of it. One is to make sure one gets admiration. That is not the way. The other, in the wake of repentance for the anger, and the Lord's forgiveness, is to see the matter in a new way! Mark 10:29-30 reads:

Truly I say to you, there is no one who has left house or brothers or sisters or mother or father or children or farms, for My sake and for the gospel's sake, but that he will receive a hundred times as much as now in this present age, houses and brothers and sisters and mothers and children and farms, along with persecutions; and in the age to come, eternal life.

People have been sent out to serve cross-culturally from biblical times. They expected a report about what had happened on return. One example is the Apostle Paul, now an experienced missionary, at the end of his third term of service reviewed many of the good things he had done. While speaking with the elders of the Ephesian church, he mentioned the following things (Acts 20). He served the Lord with humility (v.19), preached what was helpful both publicly and in homes (v. 20), did not discriminate racially (v.21), obeyed the Holy Spirit (v.22), preached the Kingdom (v.25), proclaimed the whole will of God (v.27), never stopped warning the people (v.31), committed people to God's grace (v.32), took no money for his service (v.33), supplied for his own needs (v.34), supplied the needs of those with him (v.34) and modelled that we must work hard to help the needy (v.35).

Paul wrote in more detail in 2 Corinthians 11:23-28 about difficult times: he worked hard, had been in prison, was beaten, stoned, shipwrecked, set adrift in the sea, constantly on the move, in danger from rivers, from bandits, from his own countrymen, from the nationals, in the city, in the country, at sea, from false brothers, he laboured, toiled, went without sleep, was hungry, thirsty, cold, and went without clothes. "Besides everything else, I face daily the pressure of my concern for all the churches."

As Christians we seek to do God's will and believe that "no purpose of God can be thwarted" (Job 42:2). Certain things are clear from God's Word, such as not stealing, not killing, not lying, loving our enemies, being filled with the Spirit, putting on humility. Nevertheless, most of God's guidance is not specified in Scripture. This involves us in displaying sanctified common sense whereby our minds and hearts are shaped by the Spirit of God through the Word of God[42]. We will incline to what glorifies God and helps others. I suggest that the least common method is to "hear a word from the Lord."

God's will always "works for the good of all" who love Him and "who are called according to His purpose" (Romans 8:28). This does not mean that everything that happens is right and good. Bad things happen. We make mistakes. As mentioned above, the least common source of guidance should be the subjective "word from the Lord." These "words" may be common for some believers, but they are open to question, discernment, and analysis among Christians. Biblical principles are guiding lights. Certainly, such "words from God" should never contradict God's written Word. God's sovereignty and infallible Word undergird everything else. It is He, through His Word and by His Spirit, who "directs our steps."

---

[42] See for instance Romans 12:2: "Do not be conformed to this world, but be transformed by the renewing of your mind, so that you may prove what the will of God is, that which is good and acceptable and perfect."

CHAPTER SIX
REFLEXIONS AND REITERATIONS

In this book I have sought to outline how my own basic assumptions about life and living, formed from an Orcadian beginning, were later challenged, and modified. My own cross-cultural experiences as a lifetime missionary fill me with joy as I have reflected. Undoubtedly, missionary service changed me, and I am certainly part of all that I met. When I sought to communicate my faith in Christ and my personal commitment to Jesus Christ, I needed to know how Peruvians ticked. It helped me to know that it was also a mutual need. My purpose has been to explain therefore how this missionary ticks.

It was important for me to recount that first lecture in the Birmingham Bible Institute. Pride was mentioned as an attitude that could bring a Christian ministry to ruin. I have had to humble myself often and ask the Lord to forgive the most insidious sin of pride. The misuse of, or misappropriation of, or a desire for money and wealth, was presented as the second danger to ministry. Inappropriate sexual behaviour was the third major cause of damage to a Christian leader's testimony. I have never forgotten that lecture. I reiterate the dangers here and confess that I have been tempted in all three and have been guilty of all three in my heart but thank the Lord He has kept me from acting out my inner thoughts. Nevertheless, it was Jesus who spoke of sin being present in the heart and I have had to repent many times in my life and seek God's grace again.

God, in His providence has, I believe, brought about His eternal purposes in my life, and that is good. This also involved me in research into other religions where I sought to be objective in my approach. I reiterate that I was required to "suspend judgement" and place my own faith "in parenthesis" until "creative interpretations" might be drawn. I concluded that being in a denomination was not more important than being filled with the Spirit and being a simple servant of the living God. I came to know numerous Pentecostals during my lifetime and travels and was privileged to minister in their churches. My regret is that I did not pursue those ministries at the time with more appreciation of my Pentecostal brothers and sisters in Christ.

Jeannie and I were involved in church planting ministries in Apurímac for ten years with the Peruvian Evangelical Church and we later became members of the Christian and Missionary Alliance church in Lima. Those were not Pentecostal churches and we can testify to the fact that they also grew in numbers. I could add in stories of miracles and mass conversions amid persecution and violence in the 1980s. Our contribution was tiny in contrast to Peruvian co-workers. Missionaries were present, but if we were to write down the histories of church growth, credit would have to go to Peruvians. Church planting missionaries exist but they are an exception to the rule. Above all, and without any doubt, the Lord merits the glory.

Jacob Huamán, who became both a friend and a co-worker, developed into a leader in Apurímac and he became both the President of the Synod of the Apurímac Peruvian Evangelical Church and Director of the Bible Institute in Talavera. He wrote to me recently (February 2019) and included details of over 50 churches planted in three Provinces in Apurímac during the decades since our departure, both through mission trips and local church activities. Pastor Luís Hernán Cervantes in Abancay was but a boy back then and the Lord has blessed his ministry there as a burgeoning missionary church developed. José Feliciano Sánchez, from Andahuaylas, told stories of miracles and mass conversions amid persecution and violence in the 1980s. Our contribution was tiny in contrast to theirs. Above all, and without any doubt, the Lord merits glory.

The simple fact is, that no Christian always looks good nor always acts right. This is, I believe, evidence of humanity and not a claim to final authority. Do we not all struggle, if we are honest? We do not always have the answers and we are often wrong. I find that kind of reality sets me free to admit mistakes and to say: "I am sorry." I continually repent, call out to the Lord, and welcome back the grace of God again.

SOME CHURCH HISTORY

With the emphasis given to it now, it may come as somewhat of a shock to find that throughout much of church history the Great Commission was often ignored as a source for missionary vision. The Reformers of the 16th Century and many of the Protestant theologians of the 17th Century were sure that it was only given to the original twelve apostles and that it was no longer binding on the church. In fact, they would have considered it presumptuous for someone to claim that they were doing what Jesus told His disciples to do in Matthew 28:18-20. This idea began to change with William Carey's little book, first published in 1792, *An Enquiry into the Obligation of Christians to Use Means for the Conversion of the Heathen*, in which he argued that it was binding upon all Christians as it had never been repealed. Carey's interpretation of the Great Commission has become the norm for the Protestant church of the 19th and 20th Centuries. It remains to be seen whether this is significant in the 21st century!

My favourite period of church history has always been the early period, the first few centuries after Christ, what is often referred to as the post-apostolic age. By A.D. 399 there was no part of the Roman Empire that had not been to some extent penetrated by the gospel. The church historian Eusebius of Caesarea (A.D. 260-340) described, about the beginning of the second century, how the gospel spread:

> At that time, many Christians felt their souls inspired by the holy word with a passionate desire for perfection. Their action, in obedience to the instructions of the Saviour, was to sell their goods and distribute them to the poor. Then, leaving their homes, they set out to fulfil the work of an evangelist, making it their ambition to preach the word of the faith to those who as yet had heard nothing of it, and to commit to them the books of the divine Gospels. They were content to simply lay the foundations of the faith among these foreign peoples: they then appointed pastors and committed to them the responsibility for building up those whom they had merely brought to the faith. Then they passed on to other countries and nations with the grace and help of God (Ecclesiastical History, 3.37.2-3).

Stephen Neill's classic *History of Christian Missions*[43] outlines the characteristics of Christians at that time. According to Neill, Christians possessed the burning conviction, explained above by Eusebius, to proclaim the good news of the gospel as fact, they lived good lives, their message united different races and social classes, they ministered to the needy and poor and, perhaps above all, they

---

[43] Stephen Neill, 1964, *A History of Christian Missions,* Harmondsworth, England: Penguin Books, 39-43.

were ready, when persecuted, to suffer and die. Under the Roman Empire Christians had no legal right to exist and were called atheists, for not believing in the many Roman gods, and knew that sooner or later they might have to pay with their lives. Regarding Christian charity work, the Roman Emperor Julian wrote in the early fourth century[44]:

> *Atheism has been specially advanced through the loving service rendered to strangers, and through their care for the burial of the dead. It is a scandal that there is not a single Jew who is a beggar, and that the godless Galileans care not only for their own poor but for ours as well; while those who belong to us look in vain for the help that we should render them.*

SOME MORE LESSONS

Fast forward to furloughs spent in the U.K. and the USA and then to 1991 and to 2007 again when I found myself back in Northern Ireland. It took me years to adjust back to this "home culture." In fact, I may never truly have fitted in again. Simone Lockyer[45] (a Brazilian, married to an Englishman) explains it well when she writes: "Church, theology, and evangelism all looked quite different on this side of the world." While some evangelical churches were not so good at social action, Simone writes[46] that others

> *were... good at social action. There were countless community projects, charities and foundations set up for people with all kinds of needs. However, there appeared to be a lack of "spoken" evangelism – an emphasis on speaking to people about the importance of Jesus beyond their immediate needs.*

This was second nature to Peruvians and even to me, when I lived in Peru. I dare to suggest it was easy to share my faith there. Our secular western society tends to make Christians apologetic and timid about sharing their faith.

---

[44] Ibid, 42.

[45] Simone Lockyer, 2020, *Latin File, The Magazine of Contemporary Latin Mission*, (Latin Link. Community with a Calling), Spring Edition, 14.

[46] Ibid, 14.

For Latin Americans, however, the openness in talking to people about faith is something that comes very naturally. In many evangelical, Latin churches, there is such a strong sense of the Holy Spirit being alive and at work in all things - it is something that must be shared.... these contrasting approaches highlight more than ever the need for cross-cultural mission. What one culture lacks, the other makes up for. And it really does work both ways![47]

Charitable work falls into a category that is part of Mission. It is true that we do reap what we sow in a spiritual sense and there are rewards for good works. But if we sow or work to earn a reward, or to put God in a position of owing us, we get nothing. God owes us nothing. And Matthew 6:1-4 relates that if we give to be noticed or to gain someone's approval, we have our reward already. In other words, we have been "receipted" in full, and our only reward is that someone noticed.

THE GREAT COMMISSION IN LUKE

Although many Christians think of the Great Commission as Jesus' words as recorded in Matthew 28:18-20, it is often said that there are five Great Commissions in the New Testament. In addition to Matthew's version it is also found in Mark 16:15-16, Luke 24:46-49, John 20:21-22, and Acts 1:8. A quick study of the account in Luke will be helpful to make a final reflective connection to Mission in the Acts of the Apostles.

In the Gospel of Luke 24:46-49, Jesus meets with his disciples after the resurrection and opens their minds to understand how the Scriptures taught that He must suffer and die and rise from the dead, and that repentance and forgiveness of sins would be preached in His name. He then told them that they would be His witnesses to tell other people about the truths He had just revealed to them. The disciples would begin their witness to the Jews living at Jerusalem and continue preaching the Christ to all nations. But before they went out to preach, they were to wait in Jerusalem until they received what the Father had promised them (the unnamed Holy Spirit) so that they would have power in their preaching.

---

[47] Ibid, 14.

It is evident from this passage that the Gospel has both a backward and forward perspective. The Gospel is a fulfilment of Old Testament Scripture which spoke of the suffering and resurrection of the Christ. The Gospel also looks forward to the preaching of repentance and forgiveness of sins to the nations that would begin in Jerusalem. The "nations" here (*ethne*) refer specifically to the Gentiles as distinct from the Jews.

When Jesus gave the Great Commission to His disciples, He promised them they would have all the resources they needed to fulfil the commission due to His eternal presence with them. This presence was to be in the form of the Holy Spirit whom He promised would be sent to them after they waited in Jerusalem for a while. The Spirit, according to Jesus, would give them power to witness for Him simultaneously in Jerusalem, Judea, Samaria, or anywhere else in the world. Without the Spirit they would have had no power to witness, but with the Spirit the authority which Jesus possessed would be theirs.

The change that took place in Jesus' disciples between the crucifixion and Pentecost is quite inexplicable apart from the resurrection and the coming of the Holy Spirit. The men who had once run away to hide out of fear were now openly declaring the "wonders of God" (Acts 2:11) to "God-fearing Jews from every nation under heaven" (Acts 2:5). Before the crucifixion Peter denied that he knew Jesus. After Pentecost he boldly preached the forgiveness of sins for those who would repent and believe in the risen Jesus as the Christ with the result that "about three thousand were added to their number that day" (Acts 2:41).

The book of Acts then goes on to show how the Holy Spirit worked through the apostles and others to spread the gospel from Jerusalem to Judea and Samaria and to the ends of the earth. So important is the Spirit's role in this book that many have said it should be called the *Acts of the Holy Spirit*. But since Acts 1:1-2 records that Luke's former book was "about all that Jesus began to do and to teach until the day he was taken up to heaven", it is perhaps better to see this book as the record of what Jesus did and taught through the Holy Spirit after he was taken up to heaven. Throughout the book the power of the Spirit is shown to work through the disciples so that the church could expand.

One hardly knows where in Acts to look for a distinction between Church and Mission. Restlessly the Spirit drives the Church to witness, and continually churches rise out of the witness. The Church is a missionary Church. She is not a missionary Church in the sense that she is "very much interested" in missions or that she "does a great deal" for missions. In Acts missions is not a hobby of an "evangelical section" of the Church. The Church is missionary in all her relationships.

FINAL THOUGHTS

What I believe about myself today is that I am a "traveller" and I have chosen not to sit on the balcony. The colours of my theology are those of black and blue and, like every disciple of Christ, I continue to travel. Unless I stay connected to God, my entire sense of value as a person will come from how I perform as a person and how others reward and applaud my behaviour. However, "right standing with God" through Christ, is the basis of travelling on as a disciple. Seeking the approval of people may even bring a trap and result in personal goals moving out of reach.

As a traveller it is good to remind myself of the Church Universal and that Mission includes more than evangelism and church planting. A call to follow Christ should include repentance, a call to live a holy life, but also to anticipate suffering in life, albeit with the promise of God to walk with us through the difficult times. This latter element is important because the New Testament differentiates present blessings, and trials, from the ultimate perfection of heaven.

I venture two final suggestions. My advice to the local church is that the church and its members need the encouragement and the spiritual nourishment that will come by sending the best people into mission. My advice to every church member is to be careful not to be so concerned about a dramatic call so that you miss what God is saying to you in much more usual ways.

JOURNEY'S END

I invited you at the beginning of this book to accompany me on my own spiritual journey and to experience more of what the Apostle Paul wrote from prison in what transpired to be one of his last recorded letters:

> *When God our Saviour revealed his kindness and love, he saved us, not because of the righteous things we had done, but because of his mercy. He washed away our sins, giving us a new birth and new life through the Holy Spirit. He generously poured out the Spirit upon us through Jesus Christ our Saviour. Because of his grace he declared us righteous and gave us confidence that we will inherit eternal life*
> (Titus 3:4-8).

It is not for me to write my final chapter in life, but Paul wrote another letter at about the same time he penned the above text to Titus. He expressed his hope, and that of all who know Christ, to his co-worker Timothy:

> *And now the prize awaits me – the crown of righteousness, which the Lord, the righteous Judge, will give me on the day of his return. And the prize is not just for me but for all who eagerly look forward to his [Christ's] appearing*
> (2 Timothy 4:8).

I know that, like Paul, while here on earth I "see things imperfectly, like puzzling reflections in a mirror, but then [I] will see everything with perfect clarity. All that I know now is partial and incomplete, but then I will know everything completely, just as God now knows me completely" (1 Corinthians 13: 12). Nothing can be "compared to the glory he [God] will reveal to us later" (Romans 8:18). Paul wrote of his own hope in Christ in Romans 8:38-39:

> *And I am convinced that nothing can ever separate us from God's love. Neither death nor life, neither angels nor demons, neither our fears for today nor our worries about tomorrow – not even the powers of hell can separate us from God's love. No power in the sky above or in the earth below – indeed, nothing in all creation will ever be able to separate us from the love of God that is revealed in Christ Jesus our Lord.*

That hope will be fulfilled when Jesus comes back and brings in a new creation. The Apostle John writes beautifully of that scene (Revelation 21:1, 3b-4):

> *Then I saw a new heaven and a new earth, for the old heaven had disappeared. And the sea was gone....and God himself will be with them. He will wipe every tear from their eyes, and there will be no more death or sorrow or crying or pain. All these things are gone forever.*